For the Greedy Pig In All of Us

Eat Ham.

So You Want To Be An Oligarch

A Go-Getting Guidebook for the Purposeful Plutocrat

C. T. Jackson

First edition 2023

ISBN (Paperback): 979-8-218-31025-7

Contents

DISCLAIMER

While the author can assure readers that *all* possible corners have been cut in the writing, production, and marketing of this book, sadly on this occasion he was unable to fully cut out the designer or outsource his work to a third-world Typography Farm.

Due to the designer's contractual *insistence* on payment (and the strict deadlines of the *Just-in-Time Publishing Model*), the author has therefore had to subsidise various typographic elements of this book with third-party advertising.

* * *

Welcome, Future Billionaire

"The only trouble with capitalism is capitalists,
they're too damn greedy."

— Herbert Hoover, Vacuum Cleaner
Salesman

Greed is good. So said Michael Douglas in the 1980s documentary, *Wall Street*. There is nothing more intoxicating than the endless thrill of seeing your bank account balance shift upwards. The needs of the people, the needs of the environment, and the needs of the world all pale in comparison to the needs of your pocketbook. While the 1980s are a far cry away from today, the idea of greed is brighter than ever and worse than ever for the poors. However, for you, whoever you are reading this book, the only important thing is the cold, hard cash of capitalism that continues to flow through your cold, dead veins.

You are here because you, like most of humanity, want more. And more in this instance is money. Money is how we, as a species, determine our worth. We are not measured by the strength of our character, our integrity, or our altruism. No, we are measured by how many zeroes we have in our bank account and by how many frivolous items we own to fill the unending void inside of us. We are essentially still animals, raging, foaming at the mouth to gorge ourselves with everything available in our environment. The famed naturalist, David Attenborough, has had an illustrious career narrating the lives of animal species and explaining their importance in the rich tapestry of our planet. He has only recently begun to talk about the dirty, sticky splotch on that tapestry known as humanity. This book focuses on that growing splotch and how you can make it bigger, dirtier, and stickier (if that is your thing) by exploiting Sir Attenborough's beloved blue marble for your own green gain.

This guide will ensure you utilize your unearned – and undeserved – value to rise above and steal from everyone else. You will become the king of Money Mountain and you will let everyone know that they cannot ever get ahead of you.

But who are you, future Richie Rich?

Wall Street Wannabees

You have a communications degree from a state college but spend your professional days trading cryptocurrency. You watch the HBO show *Succession* without understanding any of its satire. Yet, you still live in your parent's basement. No more. It is time to turn those useless crypto coins and GameStop stock options into true wealth, and then your parents can live in your basement. Stand up, fellow Redditor, stand tall, and stand a bit back because you likely need a shower.

Nannies

You have watched over the spoiled children of your rich, benevolent overlords. Isn't it time for you to minimize the importance of someone else? They have been doing it to you for years. You cook, you clean, and you watch their tiny hell spawn as they continue to suck more money out of the economy. Now it is time for you to suckle on the money teat. Perhaps exploit the child for your own gain. Instagram loves crap like that, so crap it up with the kid. It doesn't matter if it isn't yours, the rich parents won't even notice. Monetize their spawn to monetize your bank account – and your life.

RESOURCE OWNERS

Well, lah de dah, you have complete, unfettered, access to water, oil, coal, and/or Taylor Swift tickets. You are likely a Russian oligarch, but let's not discount those in Africa, South America, Europe, Australia, the Moon, or the United States. Either way, be sure to hoard your resource and sell it in whatever way you can. Take a lesson from Nestle, the company that monopolized the bottled water industry. They currently own 40 percent of commercial water. They. Own. Water. Fucking Water.

Anyway, you should own water too. It is a great way to boost your profit margins while putting pressure on the poor. This book will further increase those margins while ensuring that no one else gets to quench their thirst without paying a hefty sum.

RICH CHILDREN

Are you sure you aren't a bastard child of Elon Musk? You may want to take a DNA test before you read further. Or check to see if your name has the symbol for Epsilon in it. That giant asshole somehow made an inordinate amount of tiny assholes. If you are one of them, then you probably cannot read this book. You wouldn't have to anyway as you have enough money to do nothing and thus, contribute nothing to society for the rest of your days. Congratulations on winning the lottery.

For those that didn't come from the putrid penis of Tesla, this guide will help you find your way to the upper echelons of society, which unfortunately is comprised mostly of other assholes. An additional tip: don't have children of your own. They are nothing more than a drainage of funds. Yes, you are a drainage of funds too. Don't make the mistake your parents made. Focus on the dollar, not on the dong.

WHITE PEOPLE

Congratulations. You are white. Money will somehow come to you without any work needed. Well, unless you are from a blue collar, hardworking, or rural family. However, you will need to put some effort into the next few years to reach Wall Street levels of usefulness. If you haven't already, be sure to take out the competition. The life of a white person will be tough, and you will be blamed for things that you and your ancestors totally did. You will have to endure the torture of your past. You will need to somehow make money while pushing back against the modern challenges of life. Let's face it. You suck. You can bitch about it; we know you will. You always complain. But don't let that get in the way of more money.

₹ ¥ € ₦ £ $

OVERVIEW OF THIS GUIDE

This guide is divided into three main sections. Each section requires an additional add-on purchase of $89.99 to get the full experience. You can get the next one for free if you sign up for the annual trial. The irony here is an extra $5.99 if you would like to appreciate it.

The first "free" section focuses on the history of capitalism in general. It is about the desire to turn basic needs like food, water, and shelter into marketable and exploitable requirements for humanity. In that vein, it discusses the great exploiters who helped found our global economy and have taken advantage of it. There is no need to feel bad at charging your friend or a stranger extra for a piece of gum, you are just following in the footsteps of the great profits and prophets who came before you. This is religion, and you need to learn how to practice it every day. Learn from the best – and the richest.

Then, we focus on the need to develop your initial financial foundation. For many of you, you only have to work with a simple $100,000 loan from your parents to climb your way up.

For the rest of you, why are you even bothering? Capitalism doesn't help the hard-working masses. But, OK, let's play that game. Let's be honest, it's the rich man's game in the end. And, sadly yes, it's once again a patriarchal game. Sorry, men just continue to cling onto power.

The second section is about ensuring your money is used to make more money. Not only do we want to talk about making more money, but we want to ensure that others make less money. This is key to climbing the capitalist ladder to that sweet currency in the sky. This section tells you how to legitimately invest in the right long-term stocks and bonds, while minimizing your spending to help with year-over-year accumulation. And if you believe any of that last sentence, then stop here and reach out to your financial advisor in between their alcoholic binges.

This section is also about how you can cheat your way to furthering your largesse. There is an amazing amount of short-cuts to success and none of them are paved with integrity. Cheating, lying, stealing, and more will catapult you to obscene wealth. You will learn how to cultivate the shit mountain of capitalism to become a true oligarch. You are a shit beetle, and you will eat it all up as you climb to the top.

Look, you worked hard for that money. Hah – no you didn't. If you did, then you probably won't have enough to warrant the next section being useful to you. But you played the game of capitalism just the same. Either way, you need to protect your pile of gold. At the same time, you need to pretend as if you aren't just hoarding that gold like a fantasy book dragon sleeping in a cave.

The third and final section is about consolidation and concealment. It is time for you to hide that enormous wealth you have acquired through "totally legitimate" means. You need to hide it from the masses, but also the Internal Revenue Service (IRS), your relatives, and your rich peers. Be quiet and cognizant in your accumulation of obscene wealth. This guide will give you all the "totally legitimate" tips so you can make the right decisions to ensure your wealth is hidden from prying eyes and hands.

This section gives you the tactics that all multi-millionaires and billionaires utilize to hide the majority of their wealth, while also pretending to give a significant amount to charity. You'll learn the intricacies of shell companies, offshore accounts, "legitimate" laundering, and Deutsche Bank.

Don't worry too much, the general population rarely pays attention to anything beyond their immediate vision. They certainly won't have any idea on how the nuances of global monetary secrecy work. Thus, you are unlikely to garner their ire in a meaningful way. Even if you do, you can pay someone to change the direction of that ire. Money can buy happiness, but it is even better at buying distractions.

We will end with a salute to your wealth. The purpose to life has always been about whoever has the most stuff, wins. Even though the almighty dollar has not yet conquered almighty death, you can continue to utilize your wealth to try and beat aging or blast yourself into space or, if you are really desperate, leave it to your worthless heirs.

*Not just a
blank page!*

This almost
entirely
white space
is proudly
sponsored
by the
Republican Party

*"Saying the quiet
part out-loud
since 2016!"*

CHAPTER 1

DOLLA DOLLA BILLS Y'ALL: A BRIEF-CASE HISTORY

"Capitalism has brought with it progress,
not merely in production but also in knowledge."

— ALBERT EINSTEIN, FAMOUS COLLEGE
POSTER MODEL

B efore learning about the early tenets of capitalism, let's take a moment to define what is an oligarch. After all, you are about to begin the journey to becoming one.

The term originates from the early 1990s when the Soviet Union was dissolving under the hefty, voluptuous weight of capitalism. A cadre of enterprising individuals started to buy up all the natural resources and state-owned assets for pennies on the ruble. By the mid to late 1990s, they all had become billionaires and owned a majority of the Russian economy. Meanwhile the rest of the people, now in blue jeans (which were illegal during the Soviet reign and had to be smuggled into the country), were still essentially poor.

Today, the term refers to any mega-rich person as most own a lot of assets and they control plenty of political influence in their country, much like the OG oligarchs of Mother Russia. Anyone can be an oligarch, but especially you, dear reader. Why, you ask? Because you bought this book, which means you are determined to take everything that is yours as well as everything that isn't yours. For those who control the money, wield the most power, and thus control the world. But let's not get ahead of ourselves. Take a step back and learn about where all this free-market glory began.

There is a rich history of capitalism, which has provided important benefits to one specific class of people, oligarchs. The expansion – and then exploitation – of capitalism over the centuries has ensured that the oligarch class has been able to live comfortably while the rest of the world suffers under their yoke. Just as nature intended. Ain't that right, Attenborough?

She Sells Seashells

Before we can begin the glorious journey toward the highest annals of wealth, we must start at the beginning. The grandfather of capitalism is money, and money's grandaddy happened to be seashells about 3,500 years ago. Although, the Shekel was created even earlier – around 5,000 years ago. The primitive societies of yesteryear first began to barter between each other. These early ancestors even used special drills to hone the shells to increase their value. The shells were traded across the globe, with Europeans calling them *wampum*. Even today, you can see these valuable shells being sold as necklaces on American beaches and boardwalks to teenagers with blond streaks in their hair and popped t-shirt collars.

As societies modernized and the shelf life of shells ran out, new ways of trading and gouging emerged in the rapidly advancing world.

Change You Can Believe In

Long before the absurdity of crypto coins, there were physical coins. As early as 1000 BCE in China, the first coins were stamped out of metal. This was most likely done by prisoners who couldn't stamp license plates. The Greeks also began stamping coins out of metal a few centuries later. After the 2008 financial crisis, Greece has gone back to utilizing these coins until they can handle real money again. Societies were able to stamp faces of gods, kings, and their favorite emojis onto coins. In fact, Charlemagne issued the silver penny in Western Europe stamped with the eggplant emoji. It would be the predominant coin for nearly 500 years, and a sexy coin at that.

MAKE IT RAIN

The development of paper money and thus the first "currency shower" in strip clubs coincided with the creation of paper money around 800 CE in China. If it weren't for this timely invention, the world may have been deprived of the likes of T-Pain and Lil Jon. So, thank you, China. Thank you for early 2000s rap music videos.

This lighter form of currency allowed for easier international trade because traders didn't have to lug hundreds of pounds of gold and silver and it was much easier to make. This helped traders avoid their trousers from falling down due to the weight of the coins. It is a toss-up on whether it was the belt or paper money that solved the Great Pants Plague of 1254 CE.

Fig. 1: One Of China's Greatest Gifts To The World

Paper currency not only gave us the ability to "make it rain," it also gave us a reason to use briefcases for bribes, snort cocaine, and more easily pay for goods and services as a tertiary benefit.

Although they may not have had the gracious nomenclature of being called an oligarch at the time, our rich ancestors were often Kings or Queens, which was a reason they were able to acquire such great sums of wealth, whether it was paper, gold, silver, NFTs, or Magic The Gathering playing cards. Some became so rich and powerful, they were often seen above the rulers of the places they occupied as they could buy power, mercenaries, and anything else. After all, a ruler is only powerful if they can pay their bills. It is tough to rule a civilization when you have to cook ramen noodles by candlelight. The following people certainly embodied the spirit of oligarchy, exploitation, and hoarding.

- Crassus (Rome) – Marcus Crassus has been argued as being one of the wealthiest men to have ever lived. It is estimated he held around 200 million sesterces, which could be as high as $20 billion in today's dollars. He wasn't just an early oligarch, but also a general of the Roman armies, and later a powerful politician that helped found the Roman Republic. Crassus was so powerful and rich during his time that he bought and trained his own private army. He created his own military force akin to the Blackwater mercenaries of today. If all roads led to Rome, all funds led to the pockets of Crassus – assuming his robe had pockets at the time. They might have been like women's pants today.

- Mansa Musa (Mali) – "Mansa" means king and, boy, did Mr. Musa live up to that role. As the likely first recorded oligarch in Africa in the early 14th century, Mansa Musa had access to vast piles of gold and salt in the region. In fact, he is sometimes considered the wealthiest man to ever have lived (so far – you'll get there if you can get through this book). In today's dollars, it is estimated that at his height, he had more than $400 billion. Stupidly, he began to travel around the region giving gold to the people to expand his empire. He gave so much away it actually devalued gold. So, the lesson for you here is to never give away anything you own.

- Wu Zetian (China) – When you are the Empress of an entire nation like China, you can rack up quite a bit of wealth. Empress Wu is not only considered the wealthiest woman of all time, but the wealthiest person. In today's dollars, her estimated wealth was equivalent to $16 trillion. You read that right, she had as much as the GDP of half the countries in the world today. Zeitan was ruler of China for decades in the 600s CE. She was smart in keeping her wealth and power by having her own children killed. Who needs heirs anyway? They just waste your wealth. You may want to consider offing your own offspring too.

CHAPTER 2

FAT CATS AND TOP HATS

"We all too often have socialism for the rich,
and rugged free market capitalism for the poor."

— MARTIN LUTHER KING JR. (DO YOU ALSO
SAY WISE, CLEVER LITTLE THINGS
SOMETIMES, BUT NO ONE GIVES *YOU* ANY
CREDIT IN BOOKS? OF COURSE YOU DO.
WELL, IF YOU'D LIKE TO EXPERIENCE THE
QUOTE ATTRIBUTION RATES OF YOUR
MORAL HEAVYWEIGHT PEERS LIKE GANDHI
AND THE DALAI LLAMA, PLEASE VISIT
WWW.CONTRIBUTIONTOATTRIBUTION.BIZ
NOW FOR A FREE QUOTE. WE'LL QUOTE
YOU. YOU CAN QUOTE US ON THAT.)

Oligarchs have had a tough life over the last century. The yellow journalists of old and the modern click baiters of today have vilified these poor titans of industry. They have been called "Fat Cats," depicted as overweight pigs, shown with huge stomachs, and drawn accompanied by splitting pants. All these capitalists did was exploit everything and everyone around them. And for that they get joked about in the press. How is that fair?

Before we get too high on our soapbox, let's explore the histories of some of these captains of free trade and how they managed to reach the top. Follow along closely, as you will need to copy many of their actions to springboard your way from dirty rags toward untold riches.

Fig. 2: Mr. Monopoly Really Let Himself Go, Which He Has Every Right To Do

"Rags" to Riches

Some of the most successful billionaires have managed to accumulate their wealth by starting with almost nothing. They began their empires with little more than determination, grit, and hard work. They also received substantial finances from their parents. In fact, 46 percent of the ultra-wealthy started with large sums of money before they were even old enough to put change in a piggy bank. This is but one of the keys to success for the modern capitalist. Let's take some time to review a few modern men and women of monetary prowess. So, put down those savings account pamphlets from your bank, pick up your cheap spiral notebook, and take notes on how these people struggled from the upper middle class to make their fortunes.

Jeff Bezos – A Prime Oligarch

Born as Jeff Jorgensen, Mr. Bezos would end up firing his biological father when he was four after he failed to meet quotas for wrapping Christmas presents. His mother's new squeeze would adopt Jeff and give him the surname we all know and love today.

Growing up, Jeffrey was always a smart cookie: valedictorian at his high school, majored in electrical engineering & computer science at Princeton University, and at least 50 percent of the time he managed to put his pants on correctly. So, it was a shame when he initially wasted his intelligence on working at a hedge fund. Jeff certainly could have lived the high life of capitalism if he had stayed in the investment banking business; however, Jeff, an ultra-capitalist (one who goes beyond traditional capitalism to the highest form of complete de-regulation, lawless exponential, and perpetual growth at the expense of everyone else), wanted so much more.

Jeff saw the writing on the proverbial wall. The Internet was growing at a rate of roughly 2,000 percent a year, with 5 percent of that growth for non-porn reasons. He summoned his nerd energy to design the idea for an online bookstore. But how would he get the money? He couldn't possibly have used the savings from his high paying hedge fund job that he worked so hard at. Perhaps getting a similar job until he could save some money? Well, thankfully, his genius struck again, and he managed to get a small $250,000 loan from his parents. The loan allowed him to turn his fledgling idea into the e-commerce powerhouse that you know and love, which has never done anything morally or ethically reprehensible.

Jeff quickly learned the major steps toward pushing himself and Amazon into the capitalist stratosphere. Utilizing early investor funds, he aggressively acquired smaller competitors, increasing his monopoly over the e-commerce space. Basically, he strangled babies in the cradle before they had much of a chance of providing true competition. So, is Mr. Bezos a baby strangler? You and the market can be the judge of that.

Fig. 3: Let Your Smile Change The World, For Better Or More Likely For Worse

Today, Jeff is one of the five richest people in the world, using his totally deserved wealth to help the less fortunate. He does this by offering them low-paying jobs without the burdens of health-care, basic human rights, or bathroom breaks. He has continued to support the struggling small businesses of the world like the superyacht industry, luxury art auctioneers, and the space tourism market. Bezos is a shining example (could just be the glare from his head) of hard work, wealthy parents, and cutthroat business practices needed to be an extraordinary capitalist. Work hard, have fun, make history. Then, maybe you can be the next space cowboy.

Bill Gates – A Window Into Wealth

Today, Henry William Gates III is beloved by most for the Bill & Melinda Gates Foundation. To be fair, his foundation has helped people all around the world. However, let's turn the clock back a few decades to when Little Billy was just getting started.

Gates started Microsoft in 1975 and, by 1980, it remained a small organization. Thankfully, Billy's mom, Mary Gates, was able to introduce her son's company to IBM's CEO, John Opel. By the time IBM had chosen to invest in Microsoft, Bill had created a complex Operating System for computers. Just kidding, his company didn't have any real product. They ended up using the funds to buy a system from someone else. Phew, thank god he had the money to do that.

The rest is history. Bill is seemingly a sweetheart philan-thropist today and has rainbows and daisies popping up wherever he walks. However, he was a cutthroat dickhead when Microsoft became king of computers in the 1980s and 1990s.

Once Bill got to the "Micro-Top," he decided to try and pull the ladder up with him to prevent anyone else from competing to make Operating Systems for computers. He did this by monopo-lizing the market and creating legal and technical restrictions to prevent competitors from getting their programs installed on computers. This came to a head in 2001 when the United States sued Microsoft for violating anti-trust laws. The true horror of the 1990s was that when you bought a PC, you had to use Internet Explorer.

ELON MUSK – EMERALDS ARE A BILLIONAIRE'S BEST FRIEND

The on-again, off-again richest man in the world who looks like melted ice cream with his shirt off didn't quite start from humble beginnings. "Muskrat," as his friends call him, spent his formative years in South Africa. His father owned an emerald mine in Zambia in the 1980s before the company collapsed in 1989. It is said that Muskrat's father, Errol, was able to pull $400,000 out of it before it folded.

Elon likes to pump the story (among one of his many pump and dump schemes) that he came to Canada at the age of 17 with only $2,500. He says he had $100,000 in debt and couldn't afford a second computer. Stories seem to vary with what is actually true, but it is probably better to err on the side of anyone but Mr. Musk.

He and his brother would walk the streets of New York with emeralds in their pockets. Their father once said they had so much money in their safe they couldn't close it. First world problems are truly awful; if only Bill Gates's foundation was there to help them find a bigger safe.

There will be plenty more on Musk in this book, as his insufferable actions transcend all chapters. He is truly an oligarchic idol that you should strive towards in your quest toward monetary domination.

MARK ZUCKERBERG – META MEMES MAKE MILLIONS

Before he became the lizard king, Zuckerberg was once a privileged hatchling that took $100,000 from his father to start a company around the idea he slithered away with in Harvard: Facebook. Even before the loan and attending Harvard, Zuck's father offered him the chance to invest and run a McDonald's franchise if he didn't want to go to Harvard. Talk about *Sophie's Choice*. Mark had chosen wisely, but he was never really in any danger of having to work at a McDonald's. The worst he faced was having to own one.

It is well known that he stole the idea for Facebook from the Winklevoss twins while attending Harvard. No love lost for those two plastic Ken dolls. It seems that even if Mark didn't take the idea, he still would have fallen all the way down to graduating with a degree from Harvard. He would never have been able to escape the shame of that failure.

Mark's father, a wealthy dentist turned herpetologist, in turn, was granted two million shares of the company for his $100,000 loan. That would end up netting him north of $60 million. Not a bad return on your investment. Everybody wins. Except humanity, of course. Most importantly, it gave grandmas across the world access to thousands of low-class memes. In the end, isn't that what family is all about?

Kylie Jenner – Reality Is What You Makeup

One of these is not like the others. And yet, Kylie and her balloon animal lips have joined the ranks of billionaires in a similar fashion as the titans of technology. In 2022, Forbes added Kylie to the "America's Self-Made Women" list.

Kylie's mom married a rich lawyer, Robert Kardashian, who defended O.J. Simpson. Thus, Kylie came from a rich history of rich assholes. Speaking of assholes, it was a 2007 sex tape of her older sister that pushed the 9-year-old Kylie into the spotlight with a reality television show. Since people are incredibly vain and stupid, it went on to make the family hundreds of millions. This was parlayed into a cosmetic company and the rest is history. Hell, she even had fans donating money to her in order to reach the billion-dollar mark. That is some world class grifting. Except it turns out the family inflated the price of Kylie's cosmetics company, and she isn't quite a billionaire (the family does like to inflate things). Perhaps she can start another GoFundMe to get over that 3-comma line. Inflating yourself and your net worth will be discussed later in the book. Having money is great, but people thinking you have even more money is better.

If you are lucky enough to have some wealthy parents, you are already ahead of the game. The easiest way to make money is to start with money. Let's find out other ways you can start to build your fortune whether you already have a few hundred thousand dollars or not.

Before we dive into the methods and shortcuts to get you toward your oligarchic goal, let's take a quick quiz to make sure you have the moral fortitude to be a true Master of the Universe.

1. You are the CEO of a major industrial railroad. An employee recently provided evidence of serious faults in safety measures for trains hauling hazardous materials close to population centers. Do you:

A.) Thank the employee and immediately address the safety issues through rigorous investment and oversight measures.

B.) Fire the employee, hide any evidence, and give yourself a hefty bonus.

C.) Take the employee out back, shoot them, and serve their corpse to shareholders during the next quarterly profit meeting.

D.) Both B and C.

2. You are the owner of a mining conglomerate in South America. The local government recently cited your company for gross negligence in opening a new copper mine on protected lands. They ordered you to pay a substantial fine and dedicate resources to support rehabilitating the wildlife and indigenous peoples in the area. Do you:

A.) Agree to pay the fine and work with non-profit organizations to guarantee the safety and reintroduction of the endangered species and tribal peoples nearby.

B.) Fund a paramilitary group to overthrow the local government leaders and install new ones that are friendly to your cause.

C.) Bribe the leaders in the local government in the hopes they will forget the issue and enjoy their newfound wealth.

D.) Do absolutely fuck all.

3. You are the CEO of one of the largest multinational energy corporations in the world. Last week, one of your offshore deep sea drilling platforms had a catastrophic failure in the Gulf of Mexico, spilling hundreds of thousands of crude oil into the water, killing a large percentage of the wildlife, and affecting population centers on the shore nearby. The government is calling for an extensive inquiry. Do you:

A.) Shift a large amount of resources toward quickly plugging the leak and cleaning up the surrounding area.

B.) Downplay the catastrophe while doing the minimum amount of work to clean up the mess.

C.) Use company funds not to clean up the mess or fix any problems for the future, but instead for a marketing and apology campaign to fix what is most important, your reputation.

D.) Do absolutely fuck all.

4. You are in charge of a global media empire. While many of your channels lean on one political pillar, you try to ensure they are fair and balanced. Recently, a group of people tried to overthrow the government in a country where you have many media interests. The government is inquiring about your company's influence. Do you:

A.) Assess the content of your company, determine if there was adverse influence, take responsibility, and make changes to said content to avoid future incidents.

B.) Insist that your company is for entertainment purposes only and cannot be held responsible for the actions of a few bad actors.

C.) Pivot the conversation to focus on other issues while downplaying the actual event when the overthrow occurred.

Insist it wasn't as serious as the government is making it out to be.

D.) Blame minorities.

5. You are the CEO of a large pharmaceutical company. Over the last decade, your company has been selling opioids to doctors and patients through an aggressive and deceptive marketing strategy to increase profits. Recently, the rates of overdoses connected to people being overprescribed to these drugs has increased exponentially. The government is demanding a thorough investigation and explanation regarding this crisis. Do you:

A.) Fully cooperate with investigations from both state and federal regulation agencies to determine the cause and rectify the issue regarding over-prescribed opioids.

B.) Appear before a Congressional subpoena to explain how it was local and state doctors that did the over-prescribing and vow to cut back the production of opioids to prevent this from happening again.

C.) Downplay the strength of your drugs, insist that you produced the amount based on patient needs, and blame regular people for their addictions.

D.) Blame everyone but yourself, deny any further cooperation in the investigation, and cut a deal with a local judge that you paid to settle out of court and grant your family immunity from any further litigation from the government or regular people.

6. You are in charge of the largest telecom company in your country. You have close ties with its dictatorial leader who has granted you the use of this precious asset. Recently, the leader has started a war with another country. This has led to major sanctions being placed on you and your company from the rest of the world. Do you:

A.) Declare that this war is morally wrong and speak out against the leader.

B.) Announce your support for the war and leader against the unjust penalties levied from the rest of the world. Lest you are thrown out of a window.

C.) Secretly support your leader while remaining silent or neutral in public to maybe avoid your superyacht from being confiscated in a harbor in St. Thomas.

D.) Do absolutely fuck all.

If you answered D for all of the questions then congratulations, you have the mindset of an oligarch. You are ready to begin your journey toward acquiring obscene wealth to compliment that mindset. Always remember that money and profit are paramount, nothing else matters. People, animals, and the overall environment are just obstacles in your way. So, what are you waiting for? Let's get exploitin'!

*Not just a
blank page!*

This almost
entirely
white space
is proudly
sponsored by
Taylor Swift
concerts

"Ode to a Chapter Called 'Penny Pinching' on a Re-Used Podium #17"

In this daring, provocative and playful response to a paid brief, consisting entirely of re-used assets, the artist appears to be making a powerful (but also cheap, easy and quick) analogy for short-changing people.

CHAPTER 3

PENNY PINCHING: THE EARLY DAYS

"Do not save what is left after spending
but spend what is left after saving."

— WARREN BUFFET, DENNY'S ALL YOU CAN
EAT MEAL

As you can see from the previous chapter, the easiest way to become a billionaire is to start with a hefty investment from family. If you are able to do this, then you can go ahead and skip this chapter you silver spooned shit stain. For the rest of you poors, it looks like you are starting from the bottom. Don't sweat it though, this chapter won't be about saving coins in your piggy bank, driving for Uber, or working a 9-5 job with a monthly 401k contribution. Those are for suckers who follow the law.

BOOTSTRAPS AND SHOESTRINGS

The phrase, "Pull Yourself Up By Your Bootstraps" originates from the early 1900s. It implies that advancing up the socioeconomic ladder is feasible for anyone. However, the phrase actually was always meant to be sarcastic. Go ahead, try to physically pull yourself up by your shoes (assuming you aren't wearing old timey boots). Did you do it? Of course not because it is physically impossible to do. The phrase meant something absurd up until about 90 years ago, at which point it began to transition to its current meaning of building yourself up without anyone else's help. The fact that it is often used by oligarchs and their media minions to diminish the less fortunate for not already being CEOs is not only hilarious, but intentional.

Now, that doesn't mean you have to go join a commune and work with others for the betterment of all. Help can come in many forms, usually through exploitation of people, loopholes, and more people. They may not know they are helping you and that is OK. You can pull yourself up by their bootstraps. This will be discussed a bit more in Chapter 4. The key is to start to develop this philosophy around acquiring wealth. People are no longer people; they are merely a means to an end. Dig deep into your narcissistic tendencies and let them reign supreme. The buckets of money in front of you can only be gained by leaving buckets of blood behind you.

The shoe metaphor continues because apparently bankers and economists have a foot fetish. The term "shoestring" budget is a common one used by the rich to disparage the poor as well. If they were only able to cut back on basic necessities and enjoying any aspect of their life, they would be as rich as any other common millionaire. The rich still consider having things like a refrigerator, a cell phone, or a roof over your head as unnecessary purchases. It is these things and more that are the reason you are still impoverished. Let's look at some of the other things that the younger generations need to eschew if they ever want to survive in this world.

Avocado Toast: The Billionaire Killer

While Generation Z is firmly in the malicious sights of the older, wealthy class, it was the Millennials that were the first to be targeted. There is an interesting juxtaposition in the criticisms from the rich. You will often see one article chastising the poor for spending their pittance on things like avocado toast, while on the other side, business journalists will be wailing that abstention of other products has ruined the industry. Let's take a look at this phenomenon. This will be useful for you to mock the generations that come behind you when you are sitting at the top of the pyramid as well. It is important to start to develop a distaste for those that refuse to give money to needy corporations, while simultaneously being angry with them for spending too much to get out of their chosen state of poverty. With that in mind, let's go ahead and replace "Millennial" with a generic term so you can lift these and use them against anyone.

- <u>Paper Napkins</u> – How dare this new generation give a shit about the environment? Don't they know that we have already passed the point of no return? This new generation prefers to use paper towels as they have more than one use. What is industry going to do with all those extra trees? They are just sitting there doing nothing but giving oxygen – for free at that. So stupid, that must be why there aren't a lot of deciduous billionaires out there today.

- <u>Breakfast Cereal</u> – How cruel of this new generation to throw Tony the Tiger, the Trix Rabbit, Captain Crunch, and Toucan Sam out into the cold. Now all they care about is their Greek yogurt, Muesli, and actual fruit. Won't someone think of the pounds of sugar that every growing person needs before 8:00AM? How else can one truly succeed in life if they aren't hopped up on the white powder, nature's cocaine.

- <u>Beer</u> – In fact, all alcohol across the board has dropped in sales over the past few years. How can something so harmless, that has never caused any problems for anyone ever, be tossed away by today's youth? Instead, they spend their dollars on healthier lifestyles. They waste money on Kombucha because now all of the sudden they care about the bugs in their stomach. Bugs need beer too. Those extra calories will help keep you going as you push towards unfettered wealth. Plus, a delicious water-downed Bud Light is much cheaper than that $9 *Suja Organic* fermented well water that you are slurping down. Have you ever seen a billionaire that made it drinking sweet-and-sour tea? Of course not. And with all that wealth you gain, you can pay for a new liver, probably from some poor sap who spent their money drinking liquid tree sap.

- Diamonds – How can you show off your wealth to others if you don't have a shiny rock? Our species hasn't evolved that far from being distracted by shiny objects after all. Don't use the excuse that the preparation of a diamond mining area has a disastrous impact on the local environment, people, and wildlife. Those things don't provide needed money for industry and corporations. They have no value. Diamonds also have no value except what we assign to them, but they are shiny. Look how shiny they are. That endangered Indian tiger isn't very shiny. In addition, diamonds are great for hoarding and being an oligarch means lots of hoarding.

- Traditional Gyms – How many contracts that are impossible to break free from will go unsigned this year? It is a tragic statistic. What will happen to the idle, 20-year-old treadmills facing a television playing infomercials? These are but a few of the hard questions that this giant industry must face as the new generation throws more money at specialty gyms and running outside. Specialty gyms, like Yoga, Spinning Classes, and Stripping, tend to cost more and the profits go to these small business owners. This is a travesty, it is the pulled muscle of an entire industry that needs to work out and strengthen the most important thing in life, its share price.

- Golf – A game usually associated with the wealthy and white. Like Dressage, Polo, and Bribing Politicians. It is hard to believe why this new generation isn't into this specific sport. What could be more enjoyable than spending half your day hitting a small white ball across pristine green fields into a tiny hole? In reality, the sport itself is pointless. It is about the in-between parts of the ball hitting. That is where wealthy titans of industry, their bellies barely contained in their collared polos, do their wheeling and dealing. You aren't exactly going to get a hot stock tip playing outfield in baseball or while attempting a free kick in soccer. No, it is golf where you can truly move your wealth to the next level. All in the comfort of a small, motorized mobile cart that whisks you around acres of useless grass.

- Canned Tuna – The chicken of the sea. Long seen as a beacon of saving money, the industry has now seen a 40 percent decline since the 1980s. The big brands have also seen their share eaten by more "organic" and "higher quality" brands. Quality? You don't get into canned tuna for quality. You get into it because you are living that shoestring budget life. You do it so you can take those few extra dollars and invest them in the stock market or maybe a nice Ponzi scheme to make a quick buck. This new generation doesn't understand that. Some don't even own can openers anymore. What would they even do in the event of an apocalypse? Hope that the Trader Joe's stays open? Not only that, but if more money doesn't go to big Tuna, how can they have the means to fish the oceans to extinction? Won't someone think of overfishing, please.

- Pet Food – Today's generation treats their pets like family now. Even worse, instead of having several kids who can contribute to the GDP by future consumer spending and child labor (more on that later), adults today are choosing to have pets instead. Even worse, instead of feeding these pets the low-grade kibble made from the discarded muscle tissue of farm animals and wayward children, they go for the more expensive, healthier options. When did pets decide they want the same quality food as humans? And why do humans need high quality food for that matter? When pet food was first introduced during the Great Depression, it contained nothing more than bits of horse meat and old shoes. Corporations need to continue to use inferior ingredients so they can maximize their profits. It's not like dogs and cats can buy stock. Yet.

- Marriage – One of our most hallowed traditions. In particular, it is a way of doubling your wealth. This is especially true if you can find a wealthy heiress or businessman to tie the knot with as many multi-millionaires and billionaires mentioned in this book have done. Not only that, but it also provides an injection of cash into a variety of industries such as photography, floral design, event planning, and divorce lawyers. Today's generation is marrying older, or not even marrying at all. Even worse, this affects the diamond industry. How can you truly start a life together without a shiny rock after all?

It is important to remember not to fall for any of the above arguments. They are intended to shame those lesser than you into buying those things and thus disrupting their path to monetary glory. You will utilize them to eventually shame those who come after you as well. That is an important part after becoming an oligarch, do everything you can to prevent others from also becoming one. (More on this in Chapter 7). Eventually you may engage in several of them to help further your wealth, but for now, they are merely a distraction.

THE MORE JOBS, THE MERRIER

"Work will set you free" is a famous saying from the famous labor leader and civil rights activist, Cesar Chavez, about the importance of working hard to free yourself from the shackles of being poor. No, wait. That was the slogan for Nazi concentration camps. Simple mistake.

The idea of hard work as the basis for success took form with the rise of the Protestant Work Ethic, coined by one of the founders of Socialism, Max Weber. Protestants saw hard work, diligence, and efficiency as a gift from god that they must put to use. This philosophy toward work made it to the first American colony in Jamestown and has become ingrained in American culture ever since.

Fig. 4: The Protestant Work Ethic Always Fosters The Happiest Of Couples

Today, it has a more modern version in what is known as "The Grind." This asinine way of thinking has popped up in social media over the last decade with those at the beginning of their careers proudly stating how they worked 18 hours every day. Much like the Wall Street bankers of the 1980s, except with far less cocaine. Which begs the question, what the hell? "The Grind" even encourages finding new hobbies, but only so you can monetize them and make even more money. This is the capitalist dream. Unfortunately, it is not the way to become an oligarch. Working hard is a fast train toward mediocrity and burn out. If you are burned out from spending 16 hours a day selling your half-ass website designs while sleeping on the floor of a WeWork, you won't be able to do much exploiting.

While some work for fun, or because they are sadomasochistic; others work for need. In fact, the US Census Bureau stated in 2019 that about 13 million workers have more than one job. The Bureau's website discusses this grim statistic with great care, stating: "Having more than one job shows a talent in time management." Yep, that's exactly what those workers are trying to prove. No systemic issues here, just millions who want the challenge of managing their time. Protestant god bless them.

Even then, some still need an additional influx of cash. You may consider some of these methods to get a few quick bucks to inject into your stock portfolio. There is nothing wrong with debasing yourself if it allows you to grab two extra shares of Disney stock.

- Sell Your Blood – You can always make more anyway. It's like a never-ending money tree right inside your body! And the more you weigh, the more you get paid for that sweet, sugary plasma inside of you.

- Sell Your Body – The world's oldest profession is always looking for new employees. Demand is always high, more so for others than probably you. However, you can still make some good money depending on how far you are willing to go. Just be careful where you do it, you don't want any pesky police sting operation to set you back on your green goals.

- Sell Your Children – There are an estimated 27.6 million victims to human trafficking around the world at any given time, according to the Department of State. Why should those traffickers, human scum that they are, get all the profits? Plus, if you are young, you can always have more children. Hell, in the United States, you basically have to have them if you get pregnant these days.

- <u>Sell Your Soul</u> – You can always get a corporate job and make some money that way. Unfortunately, you may have to start as an intern, which is the equivalent of indentured servitude. Also, you will have to pay taxes to the government. Oligarchs don't pay taxes. Ever. So this is likely a no go unless you are in desperate straits. Selling your blood, body, or children is a much smarter and safer route to take.

These schemes might give you a little money to throw into the stock market roulette wheel, but it is peanuts compared to other methods. As said before, the best way to make lots of money is to start with lots of money. The best way to get that money (outside of wealthy parents) is to go into tremendous debt. It is time to get a loan.

A Little Loan Here, A Little Loan There

Some people get loans to further their education. Those people are idiots. Some people get loans to buy a house. Those people are idiots. The smart ones get loans to invest in wild schemes with no intention of ever paying them back. Those people are criminals. Those people are your people.

It might seem counterintuitive to take on debt to get rich, but it is a tried-and-true method that the wealthy have used for generations. What can be more capitalistic than using other people's money to control assets that appreciate in value and give you your own cash flow? There are several ways that they utilize these loans and turn them into more money. The lesson here is that you either have to know someone to give you the loan or have enough clout or whiteness to be approved for one by a lending institution.

Those that do get these loans may use the injected cash to buy real estate. Perhaps they turn it into rental properties or even worse, an Airbnb. You can also use it to buy out another company, fire the majority of employees to raise the stock price, and then resell it for a profit. Or perhaps you want to short sell stocks, which means borrowing the stock and selling it to a prospective buyer. Or perhaps create a margin account, where you are trading and buying stocks with money you do not have.

Sound confusing? It's because it is. Think of it this way, you go to the casino. The minute you walk in, the dealer comes up and gives you $1 million. You will have to pay it back, but now you can use that to gamble on anything in the casino and potentially make more money. If not, you can always just run out the back and try another casino. This is what plenty of multi-millionaires and billionaires have done, the most famous of which is Donald Trump.

In fact, big Donnie started his vast, failing empire with a "small" (his words) loan of $1 million from his father. Well, except it was a bit more than that. According to the New York Times, his father actually lent him just over $60 million in the late 1970s ($140 million in today's dollars) to get started in business. That seems more reasonable, who could truly build a successful business with only $1 million after all?

Even after you make your billions, that doesn't mean you have to stop taking loans. Plenty of the oligarch class continue to do this. In fact, when the Paycheck Protection Program (PPP) was established during the COVID-19 pandemic to help small businesses stay afloat, many of the wealthy decided that they needed some help from Uncle Sam too. A governor from West Virginia, Jim Justice, as well as Kanye West were billionaires who received these PPP loans. Not to mention thousands of millionaires who also received your tax dollars for...something. Most of the loans are unlikely to ever be paid back anywhere close to the amount that was distributed. That might sound like socialism or welfare for the wealthy, but it totally is not. No sir.

You might be worried that if you get the loan and lose the money, you'll be screwed. Don't worry! You can always write those losses off and never pay taxes again either. Good Ol'

Donnie Trump did this for years and corporations do it all the time. If you do it right, you'll never have to pay taxes or pay the consequences ever again. That is the sign of a true oligarch, one who takes advantage of the system for their own gain and never returns the favor. In the next chapter, you will learn even more ways to lie, cheat, and steal your way to greater wealth – all at the expense of others and the overall system that you use to prop yourself up to ever greater heights. If you have any truth, shame, or integrity left, you can go ahead and set it aside for the rest of this book.

Fig. 5: Poor Billionaires Like Kanye Need Government Subsidies Too

CHAPTER 4

CHEAT, LIE, STEAL

"The master said, 'if your conduct is determined solely by considerations of profit, you will arise great resentment."

— CONFUCIUS, FORTUNE COOKIE BARON

So you have put in the demanding work through multiple jobs, eschewing everything that makes you happy, and have alienated your friends and family. How has that worked out for you? If you said:

- *Great!* Then you are either lying or too stupid to get what this book is trying to help you with. If you are lying, then congratulations! Assuming you do not have any qualms about lying, then you are well on your way to utilizing this skill to move up the monetary ladder.
- *Terrible.* No duh, those activities do not work. Hard work is a silly waste of time. The only way you can move up is to take every shortcut and loophole that is available to you. And there are plenty of shortcuts as you will find out.

You may be asking: "How, where, and when do I start accumulating my fortune?" The answer is to do whatever your heart desires. However, you must be sure that you have a cold, dead heart incapable of any emotions or feelings. Do what *that* heart desires. With that in mind, let's talk about the various methods that you can use to move forward at the expense of everyone around you.

THE MYTH OF MERITOCRACY

Meritocracy is an oft quoted sociological concept, which states one can move upwards in society through their own hard work and achievements. It is a fancy way of saying "pull up by your bootstraps." This theory has been pushed by capitalism for as long as it has existed. The thing is, it's just patently false. Due to the totally fair concepts of income disparity and limited social mobility due to systemic obstacles, no amount of individual work ethic will get you much higher than where you started. Think of it like this, if you invest $10 into a stock and it rises 10 percent, you get a dollar. If Tommy Warbucks III invests his inheritance of $10 million into the same stock, he gets $1 million. This same concept goes for education, finding jobs (i.e., through connections from daddy), and finding homes. You will not get far on hard work, which is why these next sections will help you get around meritocracy and straight toward oligarchy.

Let's begin with cheating, it is fairly easy, and you should have experience if you successfully cheated your way through school.

CHEAT, PRAY, LOVE

Did you ever study for a test? Buckle down, do the research, and write a term paper? Why? What a waste of time. Part of the philosophy of an oligarch is that time is money, your time is money, and other people's time is also money. If you are already out of school, that is OK. Cheating at work, or life in general to get ahead is a key pillar of capitalism. Let's look at a few things that you will learn to cheat on as part of your new oligarchic persona.

- Taxes – The clear favorite. It is absolutely necessary for you to avoid contributing your wealth to things like public schools, infrastructure, and social programs that benefit other people. Why do you need to pay for schools? Your kids, if you have any, will go to fancy charter schools. You shouldn't have to pay for other people's spawn. Same goes with roads and bridges, why should you pay for those when you only take your helicopter or private jet everywhere? Seems a bit unfair. Social programs? Please, you never used food stamps or welfare. You only used the corporate welfare of loans and loopholes – that is your god-given right – to take advantage of for your own gain.

- Spouse (s) – This can be a minefield if you don't play it right. Scientific studies have shown that as you move up the socioeconomic class ladder, you tend to become more unethical. Let's prove that right. Look, you should have married out of money in the first place. If you didn't find someone rich to marry and you did it out of love, then you are already lost. Marriage is not about love; it is merely a business relationship. Most oligarchs and their "official" spouses never touch each other and rarely share the same room. So, as long as you can sleep with supermodels, other rich friends, or the sexiest people of all: self-published authors, and not get caught in public, it'll be OK. Your spouse will be aware of this, it comes with the territory at this monetary elevation. As long as the public doesn't get wind of anything, it'll be OK. However, just in case things do go sideways there is a preventative measure you can take.

The key is to get a pre-nuptial agreement or "pre-nup" for

short. This is an agreement between you and your partner that you really don't give a shit about each other and will take your hard-earned dollars when everything inevitably collapses. But, maybe you can stick it out. Instead of being a Steve Jobs and Steve Wozniak type relationship, why not stay together for the kids...err, no, stay together for the dead presidents.

- Games – What a surprise, those that cheat on their spouses, the market, and everything in between may steal a few dollars from the bank during your Monopoly game. Studies have shown that the more money you have, the more you try to cheat others out of their money. In a University of Oxford study, participants were shown one side of a 6-sided die and told to report it with the higher amount resulting in higher chances of winning. Those with more money would lie about the roll a majority of the time. There are plenty of stories out there about rich people trying to further game the system in casinos with rigged wedding rings, secret signals, and traditional bribing of dealers. When you are rich, you always hit the jackpot. Former president and current traitor, Donald Trump, is notorious for cheating in golf. There is even a complete book about it known as "Commander-in-Cheat." And, since golf is such an important part of networking your way to oligarch greatness, you need to learn Mr. Trump's ways of getting a hole in one too.

- School – Why would you bother paying for college for your kids like those middle and lower-class suckers? You are rich. Sure, your kid is an absolute bell-end and can barely read anything that isn't posted across a Tik-Tok video, but they are definitely Stanford material.

So, emulate your actions like those of actresses Felicity

Huffman (*Desperate Housewives*) and Lori Loughlin (*Full House*), who paid others upwards of $10,000 to have someone take entrance exams for their children to ensure they received a high enough score to get into the best colleges. Even better, they would fake their children's extracurricular activities. Lori Loughlin paid $500,000 to develop false athletic credentials for her two daughters. Even worse, it was only to get them into the University of Southern California (USC).

The philosophy here is that your kids are better than everyone else's kids because you have money. No matter how useless and stupid they are, money is the only barometer for success in this capitalist utopia.

Don't fret about the examples of Felicity and Lori, the worst punishment that they received was a few months in a low security prison, some community service, and have since gone on to doing what they were always doing, exploiting others. Hell, they are both already filming terrible television shows now. Being a white woman also helps. Have you tried doing that?

The Truth, The Whole Truth, and Everything Except the Truth

Lying is another cornerstone to the oligarch lifestyle. Many people say that telling lies is just building a house of cards that will eventually fall. Well, unless your lies involve Kevin Spacey, you can avoid any collapse in your fake life. You can start your lies off early and by the time you reach full oligarch status, you will be a black belt. You will also be a black belt in karate because you lied about it. While lying to mommy and daddy may seem like child's play, the true first test occurs on a popular social media website.

LinkedIn, Or How I Learned To Stop Worrying And Lick Corporate Boot

You will never find a more wretched hive of scum and villainy then when you decided to scroll through LinkedIn. Worse than scum and villainy, you'll more likely encounter people who love their jobs and think they are changing the world by creating some hideous and pointless PowerPoint. They aren't. However, this is where you can showcase your love of capitalism and fake how hard you worked to get a higher position on the totem pole of money. You will leave all these soulless creatures in the dust in time as they think hard work equates to success.

Let's take a look at a typical LinkedIn post.

> **Blonkington Remingade**
> TwonkX CEO & Lead Goon
> 7,991,989,891 followers
>
> It's a shame that no one wants to work anymore. No one wants to grind it out like I did. I started out with NOTHING, but cash.
>
> When I first founded TwonkX, I would work at least 38 hours straight every day. Did I stop to eat? Ha. Drink? I had an IV connected to my kidneys. Stop to use the bathroom? Yeah right: catheter/colostomy bag, straight on the lower gut. Did I stop when my father passed away, leaving me nothing but loveless cash? Hell no, I had his assistant email me a picture of his grave. Did I stop when the board fired me for incompetence? Of course not, I just kept working until they were forced to rehire me.
>
> I see a lot of people throwing unnecessary terms around like "work-life balance," "health," "rejuvenation," "spending time with family," "knowing your kids," and calling me a crazy person.
>
> Worship your work because it is all you have. It's all I have. Take it on your chin and be relentless. Keep up that grind until your bones turn to dust. #Grind #WorkisLife #GoonBeenz

You may not need to ever copy this, but ensuring this type of messaging is pushed out toward the rest of the world's workers is imperative. For when you get to the top, you want the suckers to think it was because you slept under your desk after 18-hour days to push the corporation forward. This will also come in handy later when you can utilize an army of bots - or for even cheaper – unpaid interns to fill social media feeds with more of this inane corporate dribble.

Fig. 6: Aerial shot of LinkedIn Offices in Jonestown, Guyana

Steal Their Sunshine

For the younger folks who aren't familiar with the greatest hit of the 1990s (which was only 10 years ago, right? Right?) known as Len – Steal My Sunshine, please put this book down and watch the music video.

Now that your life has changed for the better, let's discuss how to make the lives of others worse. You've mastered cheating and lying, now comes your 300-level course: stealing.

When a common person considers stealing, they are probably thinking about shoplifting a bag of skittles from the local convenience mart, downloading copyrighted music (but not Len, you buy their album), or by robbing a bank with Patrick Swayze while wearing a rubber presidential mask. That, however, is foolish thinking. You won't get to oligarch status that way. It takes too long.

The most lucrative way forward is to steal from other rich people. After all, what is the point of stealing from the poor? They don't have any money. You can take what little they have later on when you are rich and bored. In fact, rich people commit petty shoplifting more often than those in poverty. They usually do this with a "bait-and-switch" scam where you return an expensive item, but inside is a worse version of it. So, how do you go about fleecing the rich in order to get their money and move past them on the wealth ladder? Let's find out.

The Great Pyramid Scheme of Giza

In this case, we aren't referring to that Multi-Level Marketing opportunity that some acquaintance keeps messaging you on Facebook about. No, Cheryl, no one wants your fucking essential oils. Here, we are talking about a Ponzi scheme.

This brilliant scheme is named after Charles Ponzi, who in the 1920s had convinced willing investors to mail him money because he promised 50 percent returns on their investments. Even the most corrupt Wall Street CEO couldn't do that. Ponzi would then bring on more investors and use their money to pay the earlier investors. Thus, he was good on his word...for a bit. The challenge is that you need a constant flow of new money to keep up the charade. If you can't do this or investors start pulling out, down goes the house of cards. And no amount of Cheryl's essential healing oils will help those who didn't get out in time.

There have been plenty of these schemes over the last century swindling investors from 100s of millions, like Lou Pearlman (creator of NSYNC and Backstreet Boys), to the billions, like Big Daddy Bernie Madoff. Mad Money Madoff managed to grab $20 billion before the ground gave out beneath him. Bernie went on to die peacefully in his own home at 82. Wait, no, prison. He died in prison.

From Bitcoin to Shitcoin

For some of the younger generation, Ponzi schemes seem time-consuming and old-fashioned. So, maybe you want to speed run toward your wealth. Well then, cryptocurrency is like doing currency crystal meth. Except you get to keep your teeth.

I am sure you are asking yourself, "what in the hell is cryptocurrency anyway?" And that is a good question. Anyway, let's move on.

Fine, we will keep this short. You will only need enough knowledge of it to swindle others who also don't know what these imaginary computer coins do or what value they provide to society (hint: nothing).

Cryptocurrency is basically a digital currency that can be used for transactions, much like fiat currency is used. Fiat currency is just a fancy way of saying paper money that is established as legal tender by a government. Plus, it is way easier to use. For example, instead of paying $2 for that soda, you can instead pay .00000318 bitcoins. Isn't that way more intuitive?

In theory, because cryptocurrency is distributed across thousands of people and computer systems, it cannot be controlled by one entity or a third party. In theory. People can "mine" these currencies by solving computer math problems to verify transactions. If you nerd out and verify a transaction, you win more cryptocurrency. It's like a fun game that can destroy lives! That's it, that is all you need to know. Don't worry about blockchains and other technologies that this digital currency has promised and not delivered.

Bitcoin was the first crypto coin developed in 2009. Today, there are almost 23,000 different cryptocurrencies. Yep, that sure sounds like its efficient and not at all ripe for exploitation by others (hint: it totally is).

Bitcoin was supposed to be the libertarian paradise of monetary transactions. No need for a central bank or the government to get in the way. The truth is you need a whole fuckload (that is the equivalent of a 1000 shitloads in digital terms) of computing power to actually mine the damn coins. Thus, those with the money to buy that level of computing power were able to mine far more than you could with your 2010 MacBook Pro. Ergo, the rich got richer. Hooray! So, if you have that extra capital lying around, maybe from a parental loan, you too can shift the digital scales in your favor.

Even better, cryptocurrency is perfect for scamming – and thus stealing – from others. In fact, just between 2021 and 2022, over 46,000 people were scammed to the tune of $4 billion. Eat your heart out Mr. Ponzi. And since the coins are not regulated by a central body, you ain't ever getting that back. The free market takes no prisoners. Let's look at two of the most famous scams to date.

- OneCoin – This virtual marketplace made it convoluted and confusing to use, but still reached 3 million members. Here is the best part, it was never even a cryptocurrency but disguised as one. It was actually a multi-level marketing scheme. The creator, Dr. Ruja Ignatova escaped with $4 billion in digital currency and has not been seen since. Even better, OneCoin is still in use. No need for even a joke here, those still using it are the joke.

- FTX – You may have heard of this one as it happened only in 2022. This cryptocurrency exchange, founded by touted wunderkind, Sam Bankman-Fried (name is a bit too on the nose, isn't it?), who could afford everything but a decent haircut, came crashing down to the tune of $3.5 billion. A cadre of A-list celebrities were also sued for advertising FTX including Tom Brady, Larry David, and Stephen Curry. Bankman-Fried went from a net worth of $20 billion to nada, zilch. He was arrested in the Bahamas and is convicted. In the late summer of 2023, he was ordered to prison after reports he was intimidating jurors on his trial. Can't say he ain't determined.

Pump (and Dump) Up the Jams

This scam here is a fairly simple one, you really just need some influence. Or better yet, finding someone with a lot of influence to support your scheme.

A Pump-and-Dump scheme is exactly what it sounds like. You first buy a ton of stock in some relatively unknown company. Then, you, or someone with influence, pumps up the stock price through social media, guerilla marketing (e.g., through Reddit), and made-up due diligence to get the internet rubes excited about the stock. Here is the thing, the stock is a turd. The company is basically run by three apes in a trench coat and has been on the verge of collapse for years.

But no matter, now the ball starts rolling and other investors buy the stock. They tell their friends and so on down the line. Then more people buy it, making the stock price skyrocket. Then, when you are ready. BAM! Sell it all. The stock price starts to plummet, and John Q. Investor Public is left with only pennies. This is a time-honored tradition in Wall Street since it became an actual street. Let's look at a few more recent examples.

- <u>Dogecoin</u> – Ah yes, you couldn't go much further in this book before the stench of Elon Musk shows up again. If you don't know what Dogecoin is, get ready to be enlightened. Or more likely, infuriated. This crypto coin was created by two software engineers in 2013 as a joke. Go ahead and read that again. As. A. Joke. It is not accepted anywhere, it has no extrinsic or let's face it, intrinsic value. It was made over a fucking meme.

So enter the Musk. During the retail stock craze of 2020, he declared on Twitter: "One word: Doge." And just like that, shares of a joke crypto coin skyrocketed 20 percent. Of course, the coin was still worth less than 50 cents. Musk, utilizing his companies, SpaceX, and the Boring Company, continued to drive the price up over the next two years by 36,000 percent before they let it crash. They cashed out reportedly tens of billions of dollars. And that, friends, is how a sentient human turd dumped on regular people.

- <u>Enron</u> – The little engine that couldn't, this little energy company conducted one of the most high-profile pump and dump schemes back in 2001. Company executives, beacons of morality and ethics, began to spam rumors about the strength of the stock. They did this despite knowing that the company was practically insolvent. When they inflated the price enough, they dumped their shares, made tens of millions each, and the company went bankrupt.

Even the SEC and credit rating agencies (they give you anywhere from a AAA to BB) failed to do much about looking into the company. As a result, Congress passed a new law to hold executives more accountable and thus, no executive ever did anything wrong ever again and everyone lived happily ever after. The end.

- Stratton Oakmont – Sound familiar? This is the company that Jordan Belfort managed. You may remember him from the movie, *The Wolf of Wall Street*. So, just go see that movie and you won't have to read anymore. Jordan and his executives used a "Boiler Room" strategy (see the Vin Diesel movie for more details), which involved high pressure sales of nearly worthless stocks to poor, working folks who liquidated their pensions to buy it.

Jordan admitted to manipulating the stock of over 30 companies and so the judge threw the book at him and gave him a whopping...two years jail time. He was required to pay $110 million in restitution, and he has done that in full. By that meaning, he has paid $12 million of it. Hey, don't blame him, it's not like he is a numbers guy or anything.

Now, you have the methods and blueprints from rich assholes who came before you to lie, cheat, and steal your way to greatness. Get out there and start breaking the law! And when you come back, it's time to take even more from others to feed your growing empire.

Fig. 7: Doge Coin, The Future Of Currency And The End Of Rational Thought

*Not just a
blank page!*

This almost
entirely
white space
is proudly
sponsored by
the state of
Vermont

"95.6% white"
—US 2020 Census

Chapter 5

Seize the Means of Production

"Capital is dead labor, which, vampire-like, only lives by sucking living labor, and lives the more, the more labor it sucks."

— Karl Marx, The least funny brother of Groucho

It was, in fact, Marx that coined the term, "Seize the Means of Production." Of course, he was referring to the producers and the studio that made the movie adaptation of *Cats* in order to tar and feather them for that abomination. However, he was also referring to the conflict between owners of productive enterprises (i.e., the Bourgeoisie) and the workers within those enterprises (i.e., the Proletariat). He aimed to have workers lift themselves up, seize control of government, ban private property ownership, and redistribute profits. So, it is only fair that you use this term in the exact opposite fashion.

Now that you have scammed your way to a decent pot of wealth, it is time to hop up to the next big rung on the ladder. You can have tens of millions of dollars, yet you are still thinking too small. You are still at the behest of those who own the enterprises that create the precious goods for the capitalist utopia. It is time to carve out your piece of the production pie, or better yet, take it from someone else.

E-Commerce, E-xpensive, E-xciting, E-vil

You haven't read about Jeff Bezos in a while, have you? That is because he is busy selling needy consumers everything from notebooks to 15-gallon barrels of lube. In the time it took you to make it to Chapter 5, Bezos made $100 million. If you are slow in the head, he made $500 million. Even better, he was able to cut additional employee costs further by requiring all Amazon warehouse workers to insert catheters in themselves when they are working on the warehouse floor, at their expense of course. Think of how many water bottles were saved too, what an environmentalist.

There are two lessons here. The first is that having a stranglehold on the supply of products (necessary or not) means all of the profit goes to you. The second is that you can start to not only destroy the poors, but also make them rely on you. Most people see capitalism in a state of cognitive dissonance. Sure, they complain about the damage it has done to the environment, exploitation of people, and its overall damage to society; but damn do they need a Nuwave Brio 7-in-1 Air Fryer Oven. And they need it now.

Fig. 8: But Look Seriously, Just Give The Nuwave A Try, It Has Linear Thermal Technology! Cook Fried Foods Without Guilt!

This is why e-commerce is so great. You can quickly send out cheap Chinese knockoffs without setting up a physical store, paying workers, or generally giving a damn about anything except profit. The downside here is that going up against the Bozo is probably not a fight you want to take this early in your journey. However, there are other countries where you can start your own version of it. After all, did you know there are still billions of people in the Global South who cannot easily access the Nuwave Brio 7-in-1 Air Fryer Oven? Help them, but more importantly, help yourself.

Fee-Fi-Fo-Fum-Factory

Ok, so e-commerce may not be for you. Perhaps you want to go directly to the source. Get to start of the supply chain, instead of being some balding middleman. It is time to purchase a few factories.

This is where all that hard stolen capital now comes in handy. Factory buildings and the machinery used in them are very costly, which is why most are owned by private individuals or large corporations. The people who work in those factories won't cost you much, so don't even worry about them. Never worry about them. That is the great thing about owning factories, you own everything: the machinery, the buildings, raw materials, administration, and management. The workers? They own their work clothes and tools, which you can also make them purchase out of their measly salary.

Buying and owning factories opens up a variety of other activities that make becoming an oligarch so much more fun. For instance, once you have "skin in the game," you can start lobbying Congress (more on this in Chapter 6) to roll back child labor laws. After all, their tiny little hands can easily reach into that heavy machinery and pull out the screw that got stuck in there. They can be crammed into small spaces, so perfect for cleaning out smelters, scrubbing the sulfur dioxide out of the smokestacks in your coal plant, or handling the battery installation of a Tesla.

Even more fun, child labor laws are already being rolled back in several states in the USA. A great example is the rotting pumpkin of a governor in Alabama, Sarah Huckabee Sanders. Mrs. Sanders, who looks like she is perpetually having a stroke, recently passed a law making it easier to employ kids under 16. That is a good start, but come on Sarah, you walking example of why you shouldn't drink when pregnant, let's halve that number! Georgia, Iowa, Minnesota, Missouri, Ohio, and South Dakota have also introduced laws in 2023 to repeal child-labor protections. You have plenty to choose from across the South and Midwest, beacons of American freedom.

Fig. 9: Huckabee Sanders Seen Here Posing With Tomorrow's New Sweatshop Workers

So, you may not even have to relocate your factory to Bangladesh in the near future to utilize children. Plus, a lot of those are already claimed by Qatar and Saudi Arabia. By passing these laws, the U.S. Congress, state, and local governments pass the slavings on to you!

RELOCATION, RELOCATION, RELOCATION

Sometimes, though, the government can be slow, and you don't want to wait around forever. In that case, simply move your factory overseas. Southeast Asia or Latin America are good bets as China called dibs on Africa a few years ago. This is known as "offshoring," which is corporate speak for fucking over blue-collar American workers for more profits. It also is a perfect way to avoid paying federal, state, and local taxes in the United States. After all, why should you give a small percentage of your hard-earned profits to benefit the people that buy your product? They can pay for their own roads, schools, hospitals, and social programs.

There are plenty of examples of major companies that you know and love doing what is in their best interest. You should follow the examples of those companies:

- <u>Google</u> – The search engine giant decided to move a large portion of its operational jobs to the Philippines. In fact, the company has more contractors than actual in-house staff. This makes it easy to not provide benefits to the majority of its workforce. Still, would you rather use Bing? Of course not.

- <u>American Express</u> – True to their name, Amex has been in the offshoring game since the 1980s. Like Google, they have expanded operations into the Philippines as well. It seems that American companies are continuing the long tradition of the country invading the Philippines.

- <u>Apple</u> – Probably one of the most famous offshore cases. Apple partnered with Foxconn Technology Group to open an "iPhone City" in Zhengzhou, a giant city with 300,000 workers that can make 500,000 iPhones a day. The Chinese government gave the partners a 5-year tax break as an incentive. As of 2022, Apple is planning to pull some of these operations out of China and back to America. Just kidding, they are shifting them to India and Vietnam where it is even cheaper to create products and easier to exploit the workers! While the workers won't be getting a pay raise, they all will get 30 days free of Apple TV+.

Home Sweet Home

But perhaps you are lazy, and you would rather do your exploiting closer to home. Well, you can! More and more these days, companies are having cities and states bid against each other to host their factory or headquarters.

This is something that professional sports teams have been doing to cities for years. Take for example, the Miami Marlins, a professional baseball team. In 2017, the team (then known as the Florida Marlins, wow what a drastic name change) threatened to leave Miami if the city didn't cough up $200 million to pay for a new stadium downtown. Let's be specific, it was the team's owner, Bruce Sherman, who made the threat. The city relented, and it was the taxpayer who footed a large chunk of the bill for the stadium. Even better, Mr. Sherman is still threatening to leave the city. You can have your crabcake and eat it too.

It is more than commonplace for state and local governments to offer companies billions of dollars in incentives to convince them to relocate or stay in the city. These incentives can be cash grants, tax rebates, free ice cream Fridays, or the first-born child of every homeowner within the city limits.

A perfect example of this was with none other than Jeffey Boy Bezos. When Amazon began looking for a city to host their second headquarters, local governments around the country got their boot licking knee pads on and got to it. A total of 238 cities (or counties/locales) bid on Amazon Headquarters 2. Almost all of them offered at least $1 billion in tax credits (i.e., you don't have to take your profits out to pay for our roads and schools because fuck our people). Some cities hired actors to further tease Mr. Bezos. Chicago, for instance, hired William Shatner, as Mr. Bezos has said in the past that he used to pleasure himself to old Star Trek episodes.

In the end, Northern Virginia won the bid. It was well deserved to help boost the area as the median income as of 2021 was only $133,000. Those poor people had to pay for their Tesla X in installments. Not anymore, they were saved.

Some smart oligarch owners take it one step further by promising to build a certain type of factory and meet job hiring standards laid out by the government for more incentives. Once they are given these breaks, they renege on the promises and well, what is some city mayor going to do about it? You can just wait them out or donate to their opponents' campaign. In Wisconsin, Foxconn promised a high-tech facility only to downgrade it and hire less than half what it promised. Guess who was the big name that pushed that deal. Let's just say he looks like a cheese curd.

Hmm, that actually doesn't narrow it down as much. A cheddar cheese curd, there we go. Trump did the same thing in Pennsylvania with a General Motors plant, except that plant just went ahead and shut down the year after. As you can see, it is fairly easy to exploit at home just as much as it is to exploit abroad.

An Imperfect Union

Chapter 9 will discuss the evils of unions more as they are merely a step away from a full-fledged revolt complete with Teamster-approved Guillotines. However, it is important to mention them here as they can – and usually will - pop up when you start stripping the rights of your factory wage slaves. For now, just keep them in the back of your mind as Chapter 9 will also discuss ways you can prevent a union from forming before the workers can even decide who brings the coffee to the first meeting.

No Safety Dance in the Danger Zone

Lastly, don't forget to pinch a few extra dollars here and there by removing as many safety requirements as possible. But don't forget to lobby the government to help you remove Occupational Safety and Health Administration (OSHA) regulations, enforceable lawsuits, and worker's compensation packages. Little Donnie Diapers managed to do this in 2018, calling them a hindrance to boosting profits in the manufacturing and coal mining industries. If you do this then you can be sure that if, let's face it, when a worker is seriously maimed, it won't cost YOU an arm and a leg.

Fig. 10: A Factory Running Smoothly Without All Those OSHA Obstacles

I, Robot. You, Jobless.

The origin of the word "robot" can be drawn to a 1920 play by a Czech writer named Karel Capek. The play is called *Rossum's Universal Robots*. The term has its roots in the Slavic language and can be translated to "servitude," "forced labor," or "sweet dance style." The play is about a company that produces workers who "lack nothing but a soul." That works perfectly for you, as, at this point, you should realize you don't have one. If you still do, go back a few chapters, and get rid of it.

The late, great Isaac Asimov would further the popularity of robots with his science fiction writing; the most famous of which are his "3 Laws of Robotics."

1. A robot may not injure a human being or, through inaction, allow a human being to come to harm (unless they really deserved it such as playing music on their phone without earbuds, or not using their turn signal).
2. A robot must obey orders given to it by human beings except where such orders would conflict with the first law (except if the human being is ordering something gross like an odd sex fetish or Arby's to go).
3. A robot must protect its own existence as long as such protection does not conflict with the first or

second law. (this conflict does not apply to Florida
due to "stand your ground" laws that supersede it).

Robots in industry and factories were first used by General
Motors (GM) in the 1960s. These were very basic hydraulic
systems that were automated and unfortunately didn't displace
any humans at the time. However, it began the evolution of
automation and the decline of the human factory worker.

As fun as it is to exploit the modern human worker, sometimes it might be easier to replace the whole lot of them with
automatons. It certainly would save you having to deal with
OSHA rules and regulations (whatever of them are left). You also
wouldn't have to worry about unions for now. At least until they
send Arnold Schwarzenegger back in time to organize robotic
bargaining rights. Goddamn Skynet Local 502.

Today, there are at least 3.5 million industrial robots operating in factories around the globe. Automation is used to do
repetitive and dangerous tasks, thus freeing up human beings to
conduct more skilled, specialized labor. The issue is, then you
have to pay to train and/or upskill these blue collared slobs to be
able to monitor the hard-working machines. That costs a lot of
money that you can be using for something more important, like
making even more money or buying a dune buggy. It is much
easier to fire the old workers and bring in some young engineering students from out of the country. In this way you can pay
them far less and hold them hostage with an H1B visa, thus being
able to fire and deport them whenever you want. Elon Musk
currently does this with the remaining skeleton crew of Twitter
(now known as "X" for some incredibly stupid reason) engineers.

The key thing to remember here is that production of most
products will rely on robots and automation more and more in
the years to come. That means whoever controls these robots
controls the means of production and thus ensures they continue
to get wealthier while everyone else must rely on them for basic
goods and needs. Bingo.

The start of worker displacement by machines brought on a call for a Universal Basic Income (UBI) by some of the left. Most notably, former presidential candidate and guy-who-sends-you-five-year-old-memes, Andrew Yang, tried to push this issue during his campaign. Thankfully, he could never really explain the feasibility of it, repeating the same points over and over into obscurity. For now, you shouldn't have to worry about it. Not that you would have ever paid into the program anyway to help those out of work bums.

Come on, Ride the Train, Hey, Buy It

The earliest tracks for railways were laid in the late 1850s and the first complete line finished in 1869. By 1900, a good portion of the nation's railways we utilize today were in place. What better time to take control of the most vital method for transporting goods to people across the country?

Enter, Cornelius Vanderbilt. Despite the government passing the pesky Interstate Commerce Act (1887) to attempt to keep railroads in the hands of the state, he managed to prove the government ineffective (probably wasn't that difficult) and create a railroad monopoly for himself.

This wasn't even Vanderbilt's first monopoly. He got his start toward oligarchic status in the lucrative industry that was river-boat ownership. He even named his steamboat business, "The People's Line." Capitalizing on people's populist fetishes. He would move on to bigger boats, investing in transatlantic ocean liners while trying to sink his competitors. He eventually held a monopoly on the Californian oceangoing ships. He also managed to curry favor with the government

Fig. 11: Cornelius Vanderbilt, Seen Here With His Sentient Mutton Chops

during the Civil War by donating some of these ships to the Union's war effort. War is always a boon for the rich.

Following the end of the war, Vanderbilt entered the railroad business. He served on a number of company boards before doing what is known as a "stock market corner" where he bought enough of the stock to become the majority owner of the Harlem railroad. He would go on to battle other companies with connecting lines, winning each battle through hostile takeovers, undercutting prices, or lawsuits over assets. You know, the American way.

A railroad is what is known as a "natural monopoly." No, it doesn't mean that it refrains from using deodorant or doesn't shave. Although, both can be true. Have you seen Amtrak lately? What it means is that it is very difficult to start your own railroad. It is much easier to acquire a company that is already utilizing the rail lines that were built by hard-working Chinese slaves. There is also a high accident rate with railroads, not that it would matter to you. However, in recent years, spills of toxic chemicals near towns causing them to be barely livable have garnered more news. You may not want that attention; although you just have to wait a few days and people will move on to something else. Most likely a school shooting.

You don't have to limit yourself to railroads either. Cornelius didn't. You can start your own shipping conglomerate, your own airline, ride-sharing service, hyperloop, or even space shuttle company with plans to start a slave colony on Mars. There is just so much universe to exploit. Let's look at a few oligarchs who have had success in some of these areas.

Warren Buffet, Burlington Northern Santa Fe (BNSF) Railroad

Buffet bought 60 billion shares of BNSF in 2007. Unfortunately, he thought he was buying Burlington Coat Factory and was very disappointed. To drown his sorrows, he just decided to buy the rest of the railroad two years later with 34 billion he had in his couch cushions.

Møller/Mærsk Family, Mærsk Shipping

Of course the Dutch are known for having one of the largest shipping companies in the world. Given their history of maritime exploration and exploitation (e.g., Dutch East India Company), it is no surprise that this family of magnates has had a large portion of the shipping business for over a century. It is likely that no matter where you have been, you have seen a Mærsk shipping container somewhere on a truck, abandoned in a Long Beach parking lot, or being stolen by a gang of street racers led by Vin Diesel. The family has upwards of $21 billion and employs nearly 100,000 people worldwide. So it certainly is a lucrative business. Plus, with shipping you can cater to drugs lords and arms dealers easily, while still being able to ship Hyundais and washing machines on the same boat.

Travis Kalanick, Uber

Although he is no longer the CEO of Uber after being kicked out for sexual misconduct, he still has a cool $4 billion of walking around money. Ridesharing is still a relatively new industry, so there is plenty of space to start your own company. However, the competition is even more fierce than the days of Vanderbilt and the railroads. Uber has actually operated at a loss since it was founded. That's right, it has never turned a profit. Instead it has been propped up by wealthy venture capitalists, who hope the service will fully take control of the market as a monopoly with low prices. Then its plan is to increase those prices greatly when there is no other game in town (more on this in Chapter 7). Unfortunately, like a drunk who can't seem to find their Uber pick up point, the leaders of Uber cannot seem to figure out how to turn a profit. They hoped to have driverless cars by now, but since that is still not a possibility, they went the true capitalist route – they cut the pay and benefits of their drivers of course! Five-star oligarch thinking right there.

Richard Branson, Virgin Galactic

As of 2023, Mr. Branson's dream of a commercial space company looks very fragile after its sister company, Virgin Orbit (focused on satellite launches) folded. Which means there is some "space" opening up in this field to launch your own company. When Branson founded it, his goal was to send paying customers up to sub-orbital space (so not quite space). It is likely you would not want to make commercial space flight you only form of wealth generation. Jeff Bezos (Blue Origin) and Elon Musk (SpaceX, Starlink) have focused on government contracts, but they still have other ventures to fall back on. However, as climate change continues its increasing march toward killing everyone, it may be good to have a company setup to charge exorbitant fees to the rich class for helping them escape the hellscape they created. Don't forget to charge extra for Premium Economy spaceflight seats and priority boarding.

₹ ¥ € ₦ £ $

Russia: An Oligarch's Wet Dream

Chapter 10 will further discuss the wildly successful acts of the Russian oligarchs, but it is important to mention the start of their rise here. Many contribute their success to privatizing production of consumer goods, monopolizing services, and gaining extravagant wealth all at the expense of the state and its people. To be fair, it wasn't too hard given the government handed it over on a silver platter.

In the early 1990s, then Russian president, Boris Yeltsin (who was once found drunk in the streets of Washington D.C. trying to find pizza) launched a program to privatize much of the industry that had been state owned – and poorly managed – during the Soviet era. By the end of the program, over 80 percent of enterprises and factories were owned by private citizens. And guess what, they weren't your average Ivan and Katya.

It was reported that the government even sold mom and pop

shops to the rich and didn't even give a chance for the people that worked in them or managed to buy them outright. 1990s Russia was like a giant estate sale for those with the capital to buy it all. Investment shares in banks, other financial institutions, and virtually anything that wasn't bolted down were sold to the highest bidder. It was a glorious time for oligarchs.

While the likelihood of something as magnificent as the sale of an entire country is low, it is good to remember the lesson here, which is to buy as many assets as you can. The more you own, the more you can withhold from people and the government in order to gain more money, subsidies, and power. This is the true state of an oligarch. The money is a means to unlimited power and the ability to be above the law. Let's discuss ways you can ensure that you are always above the law in the next chapter.

Fig. 12: Look At Your Spouse The Way Vladimir Putin
Looks At His Oligarch Pals

*Not just a
blank page!*

This almost
entirely white
space is proudly
sponsored by the
zombie ghost of
compound interest
from Swiss Nazi
gold that came to
life due to some
kind of AI that went
rogue or something
and then it, like,
started funding
actual modern
politicians with
secret dark money
from the demonic
shadows of the
dark web or
whatever, at least
I think that was the
plot of a recent
Mission Impossible
film or maybe just
a dream, I don't
remember but I
should definitely
write this down
and mail it to
Tom Cruise

*"Ooooowhooo,
spooky!"*

CHAPTER 6

ONE WALLET, ONE THOUSAND VOTES

"It should be the power of our vote, not the size of our bank account, that drives democracy."

— BARACK OBAMA, LAST BLACK PRESIDENT

You have now accumulated a vast amount of wealth, found your way into owning a large commercial business, and have firmly waded into the warm waters of exploitation. Now, it is time to use all your ill-gotten gains for the main thing that truly defines an oligarch – power.

Thankfully, governments have greatly embraced corruption in the past few decades, thus making it easier for aspiring oligarchs to sway or outright own politicians for their own gain.

Transparency International, a group that tracks corruption using its "Corruption Index" defines it as an abuse of trusted power for private gain. Their index goes from 0 – 100, to define the level of corruption across countries, with 100 being very clean and 0 being very corrupt. As of 2022, 66 percent of countries fall below 50 percent. The United States comes in at 69/100 (nice). Honestly, that is probably being generous given the amount of legal loopholes afforded to those with deep pockets. Either way, there are plenty of places for you to shop around for the right government to do your bidding.

It is now your turn to choose which politician you want to buy! But first, let's look at how it got to this point.

Corruption has been a time-honored tradition across the world for centuries. It has been around as long as governments have been around. While corruption is prevalent everywhere, this chapter will focus on the United States because it is the lowest hanging fruit. Just remember that the types of corruption discussed are present across most of the world. It is the one thing that everyone can agree on.

Corruption has been prevalent in daily political life since the time of the Pharaohs. It was recorded over 5000 years ago that the Judiciary was corrupt. It so happens that Clarence Thomas had just finished clerking for the court at the time. The Greeks were also well known for their bribery. Religious priests and priestesses would gladly take a few gold coins from people to have the gods answer their questions. Most of the time, the questions were about the Athenian lotto pick numbers. Although occasionally, one city-state would promise riches to the gods if they destroyed another city-state. Apparently, the Greek gods still needed some financial assistance from those that worshipped them. They wasted it all on lotto tickets.

Of course, the Catholics took this idea and ran by requiring tithes and indulgences (with a healthy dose of pedophilia). This way, you could commit as much sin as you wanted and still just pay a small fee to get out of Hell. Think of Lucifer as a traffic court judge. After all, if the penalty of a transgression is just a fine, then it really isn't much of a punishment is it? That philosophy has carried on through today.

It wasn't until the 19th century that corruption truly became a built-in part of the government and daily political life, not just filtered through religion. This was known as the "Gilded Age." First coined by Mark Twain, this era marked the years between the end of the Civil War and the start of the 20th century. America became richer and so began the emergence of ultra-wealthy industrialists, bankers, and those guys that sold those political straw hats that everyone used to wear. As the wheels of industry, technology, and actual wheels of transportation evolved, so did the methods of greasing those wheels.

In 1886, former president Rutherford B. Hayes, widely considered the greatest president of all time by no one, wrote that "government is by the corporations, of the corporations, and for the corporations." After doctors determined he didn't have a speech impediment, his saying was deemed powerful commentary on the state of political corruption.

In these early days of professional corruption, there was one industry that corrupted above the rest: railroads. Numerous railroad executives managed to double-dip on construction bills and then pay congressmen to look the other way.

Alcohol also got a taste. Whiskey distillers fudged sales numbers to get out of Federal taxes, then paid government officials to also look the other way, or just pass out from the number of shots they were given.

Fig. 13: During The Gilded Age, Politicians Walked Around With A Bag Over Their Head

These examples could take up a book themselves, but you don't have time or care enough to read it. Stamps, meat, dairy, fruit, construction materials, you name it. They all were corrupt at one point or another, and politicians across the decades got a nice kickback to keep their mouth shut and eyes closed.

Then a few decades after this wonderful Gilded Age, Theodore Roosevelt came in with a pocket full of bureaucracy and ended much of the corruption that was occurring across industries. A few decades later, the other Roosevelt would also help with passing socialist policies that supported the common man and helped end depression. Whoop dee doo.

DRIP, DRIP, DRIP: REAGANOMICS

Thankfully, people have the attention span and knowledge of a pile of cave sludge that failed out of Arizona State (come on cave sludge, its Arizona State). By the end of the 1960s, the Republicans had started to gain prominence again with the always innocent, Richard Nixon. Following that, came the GOP god and actor, Ronald Reagan. Over 200 individuals in Reagan's administration would come under criminal investigation during his time in office. Unions, including those pesky air traffic control employees, would be beaten down to the tune of 11,000 being fired. Climate? Fuck that. He removed the solar panels from the White House the year after his predecessor, Jimmy Carter, had them installed. Getting regulations out of you way for profit was easy for Reagan. He appointed anti-environmentalists to head the Environmental Protection Agency (EPA), a Republican tradition that has continued to this day.

Fig. 14: Ronald Reagan, Seen Here Discussing Policies To Help The Poor

Do you want to sell arms to Iran and use the profit to fund anti-communist groups in South America? No problem. Reagan had you covered with the Iran-Contra Affair, and in the end, the only punishment you would get was a guest spot on Fox News. Anything that could go, would go when it came to corporations or rich assholes needing a leg up. Although the 80s gave them record profits in the stock market, they still needed help in using that extra, undeserved cash to do more.

Reagan would champion what is known as "Trickle Down

Theory" or "Reagonimics." This would focus on massive tax cuts for the ultra-wealthy, a decrease in budgets toward social welfare programs, increased spending for the military, and ungodly deregulation of the markets. The theory being that "Hey, if we give more money to the rich, the benefits will trickle down to the poor because the rich are totally keen on helping those below them." Detractors will say that it decreased unemployment rates and inflation, which it did. However, this is like taking cocaine and thinking that everything is amazing. Eventually, you have to come down, bud.

This level of corruption never abated, even in the years after Reagan went senile (circa 1981) and had the mental capacity of the jar of jellybeans he enjoyed at his desk. No, it only got better.

Corporations Are People Too

On January 21, 2010, in the case of *Citizens United v. Federal Election Commission*, the Supreme Court ruled that Corporations are just like you, and they can spend an unlimited amount of money on elections. Just like you. Sure, you may not have $10 million lying around to give to your congressperson, but your $25 donation is exactly the same as Exxon's $25 million donation. The congressperson will of course listen to you both equally.

This means that you, as the up-and-coming oligarch that you are, don't have to worry about breaking any pesky campaign finance laws. You can now give as much money as you want to any politician's election fund and ask for pretty much anything in return, so start writing those laws. Don't worry, politicians never read the bills they submit anymore. In fact, you can attain the services of a group called The American Legislative Exchange Council (ALEC). ALEC drafts and shares legislation to be used at the federal and state level. Don't worry though, they are registered "nonprofit," so it is definitely above board. ALEC is behind some of the most helpful laws to keep the 99 percent occupied, including the "Stand Your Ground" law after the Trayvon Martin tragedy as well as promoting tougher sentencing to promote the for-profit prison industry (also a great area to get involved in if you are so inclined). Most Republican representatives utilize the services of ALEC and rarely look at any bills they present or approve. All that matters is that the check they are given can be cashed.

Super PACs: The True Superheroes

With the ruling on Citizens United came the golden age of the Super PAC. A Political Action Committee (PAC) is a political committee created for the sole purpose of raising and spending money to elect specific candidates and/or defeat opposing candidates. A Super PAC is the same concept, but on some, like, really good speed. It can receive unlimited contributions from individuals, corporations (same as individuals now), and labor unions to utilize for swaying political activities and opinions. The best part? You can set one up no matter who you are, it's like a free slush fund! Here are a few examples that can help you find the right Super PAC name:

- America First
- Americans For Americans That Like America For Americans
- Americans For A Better Yesterday, Today, But Also Tomorrow And The Day After Tomorrow (the movie, not the actual day)
- Faith Family Freedom Fund
- Money For Those That Don't Need It

Usually, the key to opening up your Super PAC is to lean on the nationalistic sentiment in the guise of patriotic servitude. So, if you are leveraging America in your Super PAC's name, it really only means the .0001 percent of Americans. You aren't wrong, you are technically correct that you are representing America. Just the slimmest possible part of it. Again, don't worry, no one monitors these and the groups that do have little public sway or the ability to take any action to stop you. Or more than likely,

Dark Money: The Juiciest of Funds

As of 2022, only 100 donors are responsible for 78 percent of total Super PAC donations. Dark money presents you with an even better way to sway elections and bills – in secret. Due to Citizens United, nonprofits (i.e., whatever the hell you want your Super PAC to be) are not required to disclose their donors. So, you can have different shell corporations or maybe just make up uncles and aunts who give money to your PAC, and no one is allowed to ask questions. Great Uncle Moneybags McGee gave $10 million to deregu-

Fig. 15: Charles Koch, Seen Here After Choosing The Wrong Grail, Is A Prominent Contributor of Dark Money in Politics

lating the drilling industry. Is he real? Of course not. Will anyone know? Of course not.

Dark money also gives you the opportunity to funnel cash from foreign countries. This is a great chance for you to start making friends with the corrupt dictators of the world. Whether that is the Crown Prince of Saudi Arabia, the "legitimately" elected leader of the Democratic Republic of Congo, or any military leader, you can make a solid profit from them while using their "donations" to change the vote of a few politicians in your neck of the woods. The best part is it is all totally legal according to the Supreme Court! So, start sending those international telegrams now as you make headways in the political sphere, because buying politicians has never been easier.

Lobbying: A Fortune Corporate Foyer

Lobbying has a storied history; it has been around for nearly as long as America has had a government. And yes, it does originate from "hotel lobby" when interest group representatives would wait in the lobbies of hotels for politicians in order to court them to vote on specific bills. Of course, they would often have to wait until after they were done with their prostitutes. But good things come to those who wait.

The philosophy behind lobbying was to give a voice to special interest groups and individuals who may not be able to travel to the halls of government to have their voice heard. It wasn't like voting was going to do much, it never does for individuals. Some of the Founding Fathers saw this as dangerous though. It was one of the writers of the Constitution, James Madison, when he wasn't looking over his slaves, who considered the idea of lobbying dangerous. It allowed for like-minded individuals and groups to "team up" and sway government policy.

Thankfully, that totally didn't happen, and lobbying today is a transparent tool that provides equal representation for everyone to have politicians hear their voice. Just kidding, it has a wonderful amount of corruption, which you can exploit greatly to influence whole coalitions of politicians for your oligarchic needs.

Even better, you can hire lobbyists to push your agenda while pretending to care about other issues and exploiting folks who care about those pointless issues.

Take for example, Jack Abramoff. He is a great role model for you to emulate in how to leverage lobbying to line your pockets further while exuding more power over the highest levels of government.

Jacky Boy made powerful government connections early in his lobbying career. He managed to target a specific minority group that has had it far too easy for hundreds of years: Native Americans. He signed up Native American tribes who were opening (or had opened) casinos and promised them powerful connections to Congress if they paid him exorbitant fees. Of course, he used it for more important things like kickbacks to himself and parties for his government buddies. The Native Americans saw nearly no benefits, but it's not like they haven't had years of prosperity and good fortune so they could take the hit. In the end, Jack got caught, Jack went to jail, Jack learned his lesson...by going back to lobbying and being more careful. Just a few years ago, he was attempting to arrange meetings between President-Elect Donald Trump and foreign leaders. Only with good intentions of course.

While there are a few lobbying laws and regulations in the books, they are rarely used to charge anyone with a crime. In fact, Jacky was the first to ever be criminally charged. So, it remains a viable way to pass laws in your favor. But hey, this is about being an oligarch, this is about shortcuts. Why not just bypass all this legal mumbo jumbo? Buy straight from the source.

Regulatory Capture The Flag

"Regulatory Capture" may be two of the most boring words put together into the most boring phrase ever. But here it is. What does it mean? In short, agencies that regulate industries may (and have been) captured by the exact, interested parties that they are meant to regulate. This can come in many forms. A good example is that of the government agency, the Securities and Exchange Commission (SEC), whose employees tend to stay for a few years and then move over to working for the Wall Street banks they were tasked to regulate. Hard to blame them, shit pays better.

Fig. 16: This Was A Pretty Boring Section, So Here Is A Puppy For Getting Through It All

The lesson here is to start finding these humans with weak constitutions who you can pay off early on in their sad careers. Most of these regulators trained and studied to work in the industries they are monitoring, they just couldn't grab a job in the companies. More than likely they weren't connected, or white, or male, or willing to do things to the first three things. That's OK, you can gain their loyalty without doing much other than pulling out your wallet. There are plenty of people who you can emulate to help when the big, bad, regulator tries to come down on you. This is also known as the "Revolving Door" concept where legislators or regulators switch roles between making laws for companies and representing the companies. They always revolve toward the companies. And if they don't, the worst that happens is some movie with Mark Ruffalo is made and no one really pays attention to it.

It can also go the other way. Regulatory Capture is bi-sexual, even if it won't admit it. As is often the case when new presidential administrations are picking cabinet members, often times it is former CEOs or industry titans that end up running the agency that is supposed to watch over the industries. As you can imagine, it goes about as well as it sounds. No sarcasm in that, it really does go well for the industries that need to throw off the chains of regulations. Here are a few examples.

- <u>Betsy DeVos, Education Secretary in Donald Trump Administration</u> – Billionaire and Super Karen, Betsy was a prominent activist for school-voucher programs (i.e., private schools). Her brother, Erik Prince, runs his own private mercenary army and is considered a war criminal. Not to be outdone by big bro, Betsy brought her philosophy in education to the position. Her philosophy: "Fuck Dem Poor Kids." And she did. Betsy worked hard to defund numerous programs for public schools, rescinding programs that protect minority students, using tax dollars to fund private schools, and seeking to arm more teachers with guns. And she did it all while getting drunk on her $168 million yacht as much as she could. The American dream.

- Henry Paulson, Treasury Secretary in George W. Bush Administration – Bespectacled bowling ball with a finance background, Hank was the CEO of Goldman Sachs before he became the Treasury Secretary. He would go on to become a bit more famous by ushering in the 2008 global financial crisis. Can you guess what Hank didn't care for during the years before the crisis? Besides the poors? Yep, regulations. Early in his tenure, he brought together friends from Wall Street to discuss how regulations were scaring away investment. The solution was to dismantle much of what was left of FDR's "New Deal" financial regulations and others. In that way, banks and giant corporations would totally put more money into the economy that would benefit all Americans. Err, all CEO Americans that is. CEOs are a minority of Americans, so he was looking out for the little guy. He would later comment after the 2008 crash that "deregulation has failed us all." Therefore, he passed the blame along to someone – or in this case something – else. The American dream.

- James Watt, Secretary of Interior for the Ronald Reagan Administration – Watt had been both an avid anti-environmentalist and part of a group that would periodically sue the federal government on behalf of business interests. So it made perfect sense for the administration to hire him to run the agency responsible for overseeing all of America's federal land and natural resources. James used his two years in office to restructure the department, removing staff and decreasing its power to regulate federal lands. He also reduced funding for environmental programs, decided that there really shouldn't be that

many endangered species, and punched Smokey the
Bear in the face just for fun. The American dream.

As a future oligarch, positions in the government will likely
be beneath you. After all, you can control the government just
fine from behind the scenes or drunk on your super yacht.
However, it is important to note that you can influence the
administration you put into power to make similar cabinet
appointments like the above. That's called delegation for deregulation, baby. That way, you don't have to do anything while
others carry out your edicts to ensure you can exploit more of the
world for your own gain. The American dream.

Buying Politicians: 2 For 1 Blue Light Special

Sometimes, lobbying can take too much time. Legal things tend
to be time-consuming. You have to wait around at the Capitol
building, go through security, and talk to politicians as if they are
likeable or interesting. Instead, you may just want to throw some
money at these gray-suited monkeys and make them dance for
your corporate interests.

It is hard to throw darts and not hit a politician who hasn't
been bought off by a corporation. Or if not, they at least
committed some form of sexual misconduct. Bonus points if you
can hit one that has done both. They are usually in the most
senior positions.

Buying politicians has a rich history in the annals of America.
The most famous being that of William Tweed in the late 19th
century, who secured nearly $150 million in bribes through
Tammany Hall (the Democratic political machine at the time).

Nowadays, you can easily buy a politician with less than
$100,000 in election donations publicly. Hell, many of the junior
congresspeople can go as low as a few thousand donated to their
election campaign. You cannot even get a used 1994 Toyota
Corolla with wood paneling for that cheap. Although, to be fair,
a Toyota Corolla is far more reliable than a politician.

Let's be clear, this isn't about sliding a white envelope full of

Benjamins across the desk. That is low-class mafia bribing. This is corporate bribing. It goes through channels; it wears a top hat and drinks the finest blood of children in a champagne glass. It comes in several forms for congresspeople:

"Just The Trading Tip"

Did you know that congresspeople, the ones who make the laws that affect the stock market, can also trade in it? No conflict of interest there. And since there isn't an issue with this insider trading, you may want to give a few senior Congresspeople a bit of the tip so they can cash out a few measly million while you make 100 times that following the passage of the bill.

As of 2022, at least 54 congresspeople profited from stock trades after a bill was passed or news of an investigation into a firm was announced. They sold or bought stock before either event. Former Democratic Speaker for the Senate, Nancy Pelosi, has made over $140 million since 2008 with some very keen stock trades before big announcements. So, utilize your connections to give a bit of quid pro quo (Latin for stock 69ing) to those you can wield power over.

"Reelection Erection"

This touches back on PACs discussed earlier in the chapter. Did you know that in 2020, the pharmaceutical company, Pfizer, contributed funds to 228 lawmakers to the tune of just $14 million. This was clearly to get these lawmakers back into their seats after election and ensure that the rest of America didn't pay too little for healthcare and prescription drugs. Come on, insulin and antibiotics don't grow on trees after all.

You can double-dip here too, as you can use money to contribute "directly" (through a PAC) to their reelection campaign, but also to the local state elections. In this way, you can install the people you want controlling the voting districts to add a second layer of protection in swaying the vote.

"$peech Time"

This one is a great legal loophole that allows you to influence everyone from presidents (current and former) to those Washington insiders who have the ears of politicians and top-level government officials. Just have them speak at one of your companies. Sure, they will likely say nothing except bland platitudes and maybe share some of their recipes for a green bean casserole, but they will be in your pocket because of what you pay them for those recipes.

Regardless of party, politicians have garnered anywhere from $10,000 to $500,000 or more on speaking fees from corporations or academic institutions. So, get those politicians or treasury secretaries to help you with your deregulations and rollbacks now, and you can help them with their speech circuits post-political career.

"Privy to the Private Sector"

An even more lucrative post-political career outside of giving speeches is moving into the private sector. Most notably, consulting. Consulting is a term that actually means nothing. More than likely, former politicians literally do nothing but have the title. Often, all that you need for your corporate interests is their name. They won't attend meetings, provide any worthy content, or even know where they are. You are paying them for their name, but in all honesty, it was paying them back for giving you what you needed when they actually had power. This is great for attracting some of the congresspeople who often only get a few terms serving before they are replaced by someone stupider, crazier, or has committed more fraud. It is always a race to the bottom.

Judge Not Lest Ye Be Bribed

There is one snag to your lobbying and/or bribing efforts of politicians – they eventually get voted out or have to step down due to "term limits." (See: *So You Want To Be A Dictator* for tips on how to avoid these pesky obstacles). However, there is one branch in the U.S. government that needn't worry about any of that – the judicial branch. Yes, America's judges enjoy a lifetime appointment and only under the very rarest of circumstances can they get removed from office.

This is important for you as although judges don't write laws (to be fair, neither do Congresspeople anymore), they can interpret them. Semantics, baby. If you ever find yourself in a class action lawsuit, and you absolutely will, it is good to be able to get in front of a judge that is under your payroll to make the final decision. Let's explore further.

Supremo Judgeito

The U.S. Supreme Court is the highest court in the land. It is also an amazing new, limited-edition item on the Taco Bell menu... and it is already out of stock. Despite the dearth at your local Taco Bell, the U.S. Supreme Court is still very much up for purchase.

In 2023, Clarence Thomas, the silent minority, was discovered to have accepted a fair amount of donations (outside of unlimited Taco Bell menu options) by wealthy donors. Clarence, who has been on the court for decades, apparently was treated to luxury vacations by a billionaire Republican donor named Harlan Crow (who Cillian Murphy played in the first Christopher Nolan *Batman* film). This luxury included Clarence and his gargoyle, traitor wife, Ginni Thomas, taking a $500,000 week-long island-hopping trip in Cillian Murphy's superyacht around Indonesia. He even spent a week at a private Adirondacks resort that included a full-scale mock-up of Hagrid's hut from Harry Potter. You're a criminal...err wizard, Clarence. Can you guess which way Clarence leans on key issues in the Court?

Since the news of Clarence, other stories have emerged that Chief Justice, Samuel Alito was bribed with luxury fishing trips (whatever the fuck those are) by clients who had cases tried not long after in front of the court. What a coincidence.

Only Judge A Book By Its Wealth

From 2016 – 2020, President Donald Trump appointed 245 familiars to judgeships across the United States. Many of these "judges" have never even tried a case or had any experience in a courtroom. Most hadn't even watched a courtroom television drama. So, they were perfect for the

Fig. 17: Clarence Thomas, Seen Here After Finding Out Taco Bell Was Out Of The Spicy Dorito Taco AGAIN

role. Some of them were in their mid-30s and only just getting over their high school crushes. Others were in their mid-50s and also were just getting over high school kids.

Now, while youth won't come in handy, the fact that they can continue to be molded to your will for when you need them, well that will be useful in the future. Let's take for example the Sackler family (emphasis on sack). For those who don't know, or who aren't totally hopped up on Oxycontin, it was the Sackler family that pushed the pharmaceutical industry and doctors to prescribe 10 times the amount of opioids needed for patients.

After thousands of lawsuits came out against the Sacklers, their company was forced to file for bankruptcy and also had to do community service at the local soup kitchen. Oh heavens, they had to go up to the bankruptcy judge, a one Robert D. Drain (no joke), who said they could keep ALL their 10 billion dollars if they said "sorry." Unfortunately, Robert Drain, who is retired now so this book can safely say that he (allegedly) eats babies, as long as they come from chemical plants, cannot help you in the future. However, there are plenty of other Draino judges out there to support you when you poison the plebs with your products, sewage, or overall existence.

As of this writing, the Sackler case is being retried, but the point is that you should start buying judges, now. As your wealth continues to balloon and you affect more people negatively, you will face more lawsuits, more people yelling at you with clever signs (meh, who cares), and more Congressional subpoenas (meh, who cares). All you will need to do is have your 100 or so lawyers find the right place to have the case "judged" by someone that you already paid to have appointed to the position. Ta Da! Plant some seeds, and you get – only you – get to truly reap the rewards.

Let's mention one additional benefit to having bought your own judiciary. It comes back to our good friend, Donnie Trump. Throw out the government that you don't like!

ARE YOU **SICK AND TIRED** OF HAVING YOUR VOTE COUNTED THE SAME AS YOUR FELLOW CITIZEN WHO YOU DON'T *SHARE THE SAME VIEWS AS?*

Are you *fed up* with having to accept legitimate results of democratic processes that **YOU** participate in?

Are you ready to throw off the chains of the Constitution and just say *FUCK IT* to more than half of your fellow countrypeople?

Then come on down to **CHEAP JUDGES EMPORIUM AND JERKY STORE!**

We have *plenty* of installed judges that are easy to sway your way on even the most seditious of charges. Our judges really don't give a shit about the law! *Some even can't **read** it!*

But, while you are here, grab some jerky for **30% OFF**. We have beef, pork, and former, deceased Judge Scalia jerky available at **rock bottom prices!**

STILL MORE EXPENSIVE THAN OUR JUDGES, BUT IF *YOU* BUY 1KG OF JERKY TODAY, YOU'LL GET TWO KENTUCKY JUDGES **FOR THE PRICE OF ONE!**

Yes, that is right. You can promote the overthrow of a democratic election and find it legitimate with judges. If, or when, they fail, it will fall on your political puppet. You will barely even be mentioned in the news. A big part of that is that you should own some of the media at this point. Let's talk about that now, as owning the "fourth branch of government" is the final branch you need to complete your oligarchic takeover of the country.

As said before, politicians come and go. It is usually not a long-term investment. And judges, well, they are something you need, but they cannot exactly influence much beyond the wood-stained podiums of their courtrooms. No, what you need is to influence the strongest political power of any nation. The media.

LIGHTS, CAMERA, DISTRACTION

There was a time when the media was used to fight against exploitation, injustice, and abuses of human rights. It fought and won against colonialism, racism, and apartheid. Thankfully, that is in the past. Now, you can utilize the arm of the media to fight FOR exploitation and injustice. Whether it is television, radio, podcasts, social media, or semaphore, the world of mass media is your oyster. So let's get shucking.

IT'S NOT TV, IT'S HBOLIGARCHY

Once upon a time, a long, long time ago, there were many different television networks. Some were owned by big companies, some owned by small ones, some even went off air at the end of the day. Imagine not being able to watch the same five headlines regurgitated by CNN late into the evening. Horrible. Luckily, the world was saved over the past few decades with the concentration of media ownership. Now, only a few companies own the vast majority of all media. This is what is known as an oligopoly. Yep, that's right, just monopoly + oligarch. A beautiful pairing.

This concentration was caused by our good friend, deregulation, which removed barriers to media mergers as well as insurances to keep media diversified. And nobody likes diversity. In the early 1980s, 90 percent of the media in the United States was controlled by 50 companies. By 2011, only six companies were left that controlled it. Those companies are GE (Comcast, NBC), News-Corp (Fox), Disney (ABC, ESPN), Viacom (MTV), Time Warner (CNN), and CBS (Showtime). Unless you are wasting your time watching public broadcasting (paid for viewers that hopefully aren't you), then you are watching movies under the watchful eye of one of these six companies.

So, what does this mean for you? Well, it means you need to get in on this cable cash cow. Ideally, you want to focus on taking over a network, or building your own. This isn't really about the money though. This is about the power the media has over your common poors and whatever is left of the middle class. With a network consisting of half-wit "journalists" and communications majors, you can control the narrative of any issue you want and how potential voters think about it. (More on this in Chapter 9). In addition, you can utilize a firehose of streaming content or basic cable programming to keep them occupied and docile. Plus, maybe Brian Cox could play you in an HBO show. That would be pretty cool.

NPR's This American Oligarch

You may be asking, "Who gives a shit about the radio?" And the answer would be, "No one, maybe the blind?" However, over the last decade, the rise of the podcast has made utilizing your ears popular again.

While the radio space is not nearly as concentrated as television, mostly due to the sheer amount of radio stations across the United States, there are still several top dogs such as Sinclair Media Group and iHeartMedia. While they have been focused mostly on the traditional FM/AM areas, big conglomerates are starting to turn their greedy little acquisition hands towards the juicy landscape of podcasts. In fact, iHeart already has 800 active shows reaching over 30 million listeners. And only 780 of them are true crime podcasts.

It is yet to be seen if the podcast phenomenon will last, but you might as well grab a few hundred podcasts and have them start spewing exploitative garbage for you. Joe Rogan is always up for it.

@Oligarch23587

The crown-brown jewel of the media landscape, this is likely where you will still have the most opportunities at building an empire as the landscape is still open and relatively new compared to television and radio.

As attention spans have dwindled, so has the quality and quantity of content presented in order to keep the eyes focused on something for more than eight seconds. So, if you made it this far, congratulations! Facebook (including Instagram), Twitter (X), and now, Tik Tok have become the Triumvirate of Crap. Facebook and Twitter were the numbers 1 and 3 with the most likely sources of fake news stories (as of 2017).

That means if you are able to take over or make a similar, mostly useless, social media platform of your own, you can easily pump out hundreds of memes and fake stories to influence the audience to whatever you want. Dictators have used this successfully during elections in third world countries like Myanmar, Ethiopia, and America. And you will be more powerful than a dictator soon enough. You might be able to save a few bucks, instead of bribing a congressperson, just hire an Eastern European group of teens to make some Facebook memes that ensure the congressperson loses their election. Then you can install a cheaper lackey. Always look for ways to cut costs.

Speaking of cutting costs, if you do buy a social media company, you might want to know how to use it, or monetize it, or ensure you can wipe your own ass. Case in point, Elon Musk, who likely cannot do any of those things. This billionaire manbaby who was addicted to Twitter, decided to buy it for $44 billion in 2022. It is estimated that he paid twice what Twitter was worth, other estimates say he paid $44 billion too much for it. It is like if your overweight, Christofacist cousin bought

Chick-fil-A, or if your alcoholic, deadbeat dad bought Build-A-Bear. Even worse, the man-child lost his spot as the number 1 richest person in the world as of March 2023. Either way, you don't want to make the same mistake he did. Be sure to do your due diligence, be anonymous, make a fair offer, and determine what are the best memes you can use on the platform to further your agenda.

A Whole New World To Exploit

Did you know that there are other countries besides the United States? Shocking. Did you also know that they have their fair share of wonderful oligarchs and exploiters? It's true! Let's take a brief private jet flight around to see some of the great stuff they are doing in other parts of the globe.

China: From Red Dragon to Gold Dragon

It was 50 years ago that China was still considered a mostly agrarian society. The vast majority of the population lived in the rural west and China had only a few cities with populations that rivaled industrialized countries. Yet, by 2011, China had more than 140 billionaires. And as of 2022, there were 1,133 billionaires. Meanwhile, the United States has a measly 716. Everyone knows that whichever country has the most billionaires by the end, wins. Many of China's billionaires made their wealth in real estate, mostly by building huge skyscraper apartment complexes that no one ever lived in. You know, giving back to the community. While the Communist party remains the sole power in the country, a majority of the top party leaders certainly aren't living off a government salary. Several billionaire party members have unfortunately "disappeared" in the past decade under Xi JinPooh's regime. So, best not to conduct your oligarchic desires in East Asia for now. Otherwise, Pooh's gonna get ya.

TURKEY: A EUROPEAN AND ASIAN OLIGARCHY

Since a military coup in 1960, Turkey has had a small group of oligarchs formed from some of the historically elite families in the country. While their power waned when Recep Tayyip Erdogan was elected, he has since changed his tune and learned to love the oligarchs. He has done this by beginning to court the many Russian oligarchs who have had to flee sanctions due to the war in Ukraine. These poor oligarchs, much like migrants from Africa, have abandoned their homes and risked the open waters on their boats to find a safe haven. Of course, their boats were just a bit bigger than the migrants fleeing from North Africa, but that is just splitting hairs.

SAUDI ARABIA: AN OLIGARCHIC OASIS

The Kingdom has a rich history of oligarchy. In fact, you can say it's basically the entire history of the country since 1932. As the country is ruled by the royal family, it has the rare distinction of combining government leaders who are all oligarchs – business WITH pleasure. The entire House of Saud is supposedly composed of 15,000 members, but really only about 1500 have true power and enough wealth to back it up. Of those 1500, only about 1500 are men. Sorry ladies, but hey, at least you aren't a journalist. That definitely won't cut it in Saudi Arabia.

RUSSIA: THE GRAND DADDY OF OLIGARCHS

As mentioned earlier, Russia has maybe been the most successful in cultivating a rich, oligarch class. There are documented cases of oligarchs as far back as the 15th century. But it was the fall of the Soviet Union that truly brought these champions out. As the Iron Curtain fell, a small group of already wealthy individuals launched themselves into the stratosphere by gaining control and divvying up the vast resources and utilities that were no longer under state control. These new oligarchs of the 90s, which coincidentally was also the name of the boy band they started, used their power to finance the politicians they wanted ruling the new Russian "democracy." This included the reelection of Boris Yeltsin in 1996, who had first ushered in the fall of the Soviet Union. These OG oligarchs and new ones helped push Vladimir Putin into power when Yeltsin resigned in 1999. They have since controlled the result of most elections, whether by rigging the actual vote or even removing any opposition candidate who may provide even an inkling of a chance to win. At the same time, they have been able to exponentially grow their wealth with control of resources and utilities, usually siphoning off as much profit as they can to keep Putin happy and the people firmly under their golden valenki (boots).

Fig. 18: Before BTS, One Direction, and The Backstreet Boys.

VENEZUELA: YOU CAN'T SPELL OLIGARCH WITHOUT OIL

Venezuela dived headfirst into oligarchy when they elected Hugo Chavez in 1998. Once hailed as a revolutionary, he had championed socialism for the people during his campaign run. His slogan was "Motherland, Socialism, or Death." Not bad, but he lost some voters because he forgot to include "Pizza Parties" in it. Chavez's policies – and lack of sufficient pizza parties – tanked the economy over the years. In addition, rampant corruption coupled with excessive pizza consumption by the old elite class further increased the divide between the poor and the rich. Chavez would turn on these old oligarchs to...start a new oligarchy, with blackjack and hookers. They were known as the "bolichicos" who leveraged additional corruption and political favors to capture wealth and natural resources, particularly given Venezuela's vast oil deposits. In 2019, Chavez's replacement, Nicolas Maduro, attempted economic reform by changing the socialist economy into a free market economy. Why anyone thought they were ever a socialist economy is a head scratcher. This further tanked the economy and increased inequity. But who cares, the bolichicos were able to get richer. They will be eating golden crusted pizzas for a long time.

Now you know how to successfully utilize your wealth to tip the scales of power to your favor. If you play your politicians right – and you will – you won't have to worry about any pesky government getting in your way as you continue your march toward complete domination. However, as you have read, there are others out there with the same mindset. Your competitors. Some are your peers, for now. They are trying to make it to the top. You cannot let that happen. It is time to learn how to crush your competition into submission.

These #Statues have been consolidated into the Private Collection™ of Goon Beenz Ltd©, a subsidiary of WeHoard. We kindly ask you to get off our property. #CoolBeenz

CHAPTER 7

CRUSH THE COMPETITION

"Capitalism and competition are opposites."

— PETER THIEL, FACEBOOK INVESTOR AND
LIBERTARIAN WHACK JOB

Congratulations, you have reached the top .0001 percent of the population in terms of wealth. Don't get too smug. The first 99.99 percent is fairly easy to get past after you've stepped over plebs, friends, family, the middle class, homeless children, pensioners, and immigrants. You've bought politicians, factories, media outlets, and a snazzy new top hat to complete your look. Now you face the toughest test of your "career." Don't worry, though, you will still have plenty of opportunities to step over these lesser monetary mortals while battling the other captains of industry to become the one true oligarch.

REAL LIFE MONOPOLY

When you consider your competition, take the same attitude toward them that you do your family and friends when playing monopoly. That attitude should be to completely crush them by any means necessary while berating them incessantly, especially the children. Unfortunately, if things aren't going your way, you cannot just flip the board and walk off. Just kidding, you totally can. There are several methods that are at your disposal – especially with all your disposable income – that you can use against your competition. Many of these actually aren't that far off from the game, while some are a bit more advanced than those lazy Parker Bros.

If You Can't Beat 'Em, Buy 'Em

The original philosophy of capitalism was the promotion of healthy competition between firms for customers, which would lead to lower prices, better quality products and services, a greater variety of said products and services, and more innovation across industries. Capitalism, in fact, has lifted more people out of poverty than any other economic system. So, suck it socialism.

However, that was the capitalism of the olden days, with stupid people dreaming to make the world a better place for everyone. Yuck. Thankfully, America in its infancy, said that was totally pointless and began the march toward monopoly. Colonists began to award exclusive contracts to companies to help build the New World in the late 17th and early 18th centuries. These organizations, like "The Virginia Company," "The Massachusetts Bay Company," "Ye Olde Amazone," and "The Disney East India Company" all made massive profits during this time.

Fig. 19: Our Capitalist Forefathers, After Realizing It Was Easier To Exploit The People Rather Than Help Them

By the late 19th century and into the early 20th century, major assets like steel, oil, and railroads became dominated by a few select companies. The government has been fighting against monopolies since this time. They would pass anti-trust bills to breakup monopolies; the early examples being Standard Oil and American Tobacco. Later, as technology firms became the new oil, AT&T was forced to break up. Don't fret though, for every monopoly the government breaks up, new ones pop up in other industries. The government is like a kid with poor depth perception and a lazy eye trying to win Whack-A-Mole. He just ain't going to be very successful.

Which brings us to today, where monopolies, oligopolies, or "near monopolies" (companies that own most of the industry, like De Beers with diamonds) are thriving under a massively deregulated system.

As discussed earlier, when you are first starting out with your company and of course a loan from your parents, you will embrace the competitive, innovative nature that capitalism affords you. This gives you the opportunity to build better quality products or develop more efficient services for a particular industry and customer base. You likely won't even turn a profit for those first few years of your company, but you'll gain more of the market share. But what happens when you get to the top of your industry? What do you do when you have beaten out the other startups and small businesses that you were competing against when you were a fledgling company? You do what any good capitalist, oligarch, or conservative would do. You pull that fucking ladder up with you. So, how does one do this? Let's discuss the first way: Mergers and Acquisitions.

If you are too dim to understand either of those words, even with all the context clues from the book so far, let's briefly go over what Mergers and Acquisitions – or M&A (as it is known by insufferable business majors) – means.

- **Merger:** When two companies combine to create a larger, joint venture (i.e., company).
- **Acquisition:** When one company takes over another company and all its assets.

Fig. 20: MBA Graduates Discussing Business Mergers And Acquisitions

There, you now have a master's in business administration (MBA). You are the equivalent of a monkey in a business suit. So, what does this mean for you? Well, now that you are at or near the top, it is time to go against everything that helped you get this far. The old theories of capitalism that brought you up this ladder are dead to you. You are a born-again capitalist: crazier and frothing at the mouth like a feral mongoose.

The basic tenet of being a feral mongoose is to use your excessive wealth and share of the market to buy out any other company that threatens your kingdom. As discussed in an earlier chapter, you should by now be using inferior materials for your products, cutting benefits to provided services, and raising prices for a customer base who has no other options. In this position, there will be new companies, often called "disrupters," that may threaten you or the entire way the industry is run. This is no bueno. So, rather than appealing to the better angels of another company's nature, appeal to their CEO's greed. The technology giants of Silicon Valley provide no better example of this philosophy.

In 2021 alone, Amazon, Google, Facebook, Apple, and Microsoft had bought up dozens of smaller firms between them. In the decade before that, they bought up over 600 startups. The Federal Trade Commission (FTC) has not been able to keep up and determine the legality of most of these purchases. So, you won't have to worry about the government getting in your way as you buy out any competitor, no matter how small they appear. Stamp out the competition in its infancy, much like a king does to a legitimate heir, or how actors & actresses name their kids poorly, so they won't outshine them in the future.

Ok, but that is the small fish. When it comes to the bigger tilapia in the river, you'll want to turn to mergers. You need to ensure you truly have an iron grip on the market when approaching these to utilize on rival companies. That way you can take your rivals over and remove any trace of their brand, CEO, or quality when you take over their assets. For instance, do you know who Morgan Stanley is? Sure you do. Do you know who Dean Witter is? The fuck you do. Guess who took over whom? Dow Chemical did something similar to Union Carbide, both were wonderfully romantic, flowery names for chemical production companies. Dow Chemical won out, although "Dow's Lily Cellulose Resin and Ethylene Oxide" was a close compromise between the two.

The method of starting the process of a merger is when a company buys a large amount of the other's assets – usually to the point they have a majority of the other company – which allows them to buy the rest of it or "merge." You may remember a certain railroad tycoon discussed earlier that did exactly this to ensure he owned all four of the railroads in his monopoly game and in real life. Which means, exercise your immense wealth and the free market to just slip in and buy up your competitors via their stock offerings on Wall Street, then you take everything they have on Main Street. Look at you now, you are your very own Patrick Bateman, an *American Psycho*.

To Catch A Predator

OK, so Mergers & Acquisitions sounds like a lot of work and your competitors may actually get something out of it. Even if you win, is that really enough? Don't you want to crush them into the poor house? Of course you do, or you wouldn't be here. So let's look at another strategy that may quench that thirst for bankruptcy bloodlust: predatory pricing.

In the most simplistic of terms, predatory pricing is when a company sets the price for a product or service obscenely low in order to undermine any other competitors in the marketplace. In the short term, the company often takes a massive loss. However, this allows them to conquer more of the customer base. The customers, now loyal to this company, will not want to switch to a competitor.

The final stage is that the company increases their prices at an exponential rate and these customers will pay the increase because it is easier to keep the product or service. Competitors can no longer keep up as they have too few customers. They have plenty of supply, but little demand and are forced to exit the market or be bought out by the

Fig. 21: Even Arnold Schwarzenegger Struggled Against Predatory Pricing

bigger fish (i.e., you if you do this right). The predator company ends up charging more for the product or service then what the customers would have paid if competition continued to exist in the specific marketplace. Thus, the predator company just ate all of the industry food chain. If the competition bleeds money, you can kill it.

It may seem counterintuitive – and maybe a bit scary – to lose money in the early run of this strategy. You are right to be a bit skeptical as it isn't 100 percent effective. However, once you get past the first stage of predation, then the second stage of recoupment is where you will see the fruits of your labor. Yes, delayed gratification seems silly when you are becoming an oligarch, but you only have to do it once or twice and then never again. Think of it like eating vegetables, you only have to eat broccoli once and then you can eat all the macaroni and cheese you want forever without any consequences. Don't listen to doctors on this advice, just believe it. It is all about short term results.

There are plenty of companies that have or are currently participating in this type of business practice.

WALMART & TARGET: ALL DRUGS ARE GOOD DRUGS

This occurred in Minnesota. The spineless state government decided to set a price floor for prescription drug costs. These drugs included birth control pills set at $9 for a one-month supply. Walmart, being of sound mind and not giving a shit what any government says, decided to drastically undercut the price of many of these drugs. Target was then like, "Aw hell nah, you ain't taking the twin cities from us" (pretty sure this was the verbatim letter to Walmart), decided to match these lower prices. Both companies were in violation of the government price floor. The unfortunate part about this war is that consumers ended up winning with the low prices of generic prescription drugs (around $4.00). This is likely because the big companies fought it out for the chance to gain a monopoly on prescription drugs. It is almost as if this was a form of capitalism that worked for real people. However, the companies were able to bill the hospitals and local pharmacies, so they didn't lose much profit. Let's look at an example of when predatory pricing worked more in favor of the predator.

AMAZON: A BOOK A DAY KEEPS THE PROFITS AWAY FROM OTHERS

You probably bought this book on Amazon, well, beggars and authors cannot be choosers. Hell, they can only be supermarket bag boys and girls at this point. Amazon controls the market for self-published authors and even most published authors with their ability to provide an easy market to sell books. We are talking about a 90 percent share with book sales. There is no place else to go, even after you market to Barnes & Noble and small bookstores, Amazon still reigns supreme with access and price. They did this by keeping their prices incredibly low when they first emerged in the late 90s. In fairly short order, smaller bookstores fell like dominoes as they could not compete with the price and convenience of the Bozo's e-bookstore. You can see the documentary about this known as *You've Got Mail.*

Air Canada: Sorry Airlines

While Canadians are well known for their apologies, they still are just several kilometers (or a few freedom miles) away from being American assholes. Air Canada decided to lower the prices of their tickets to around – or even below – that of the budget airlines that were trying to compete in the Canadian market. The year prior, Air Canada had acquired Canadian Airlines in what analysts called, "the most boring acquisition ever." Since then, Air Canada has tried to undercut the others with the hopes of capturing the juicy Montreal to Halifax route. Unfortunately, the government came in and stopped them from conquering the entire eastern Canadian flight route (i.e., the famed Moose Route).

Uber: Rate Me Baby

If you are reading this, it is likely that you have hailed an Uber at least once, or vomited in an Uber at least once, or had an Uber driver try to rape you at least once, or you got a cute little Deer Park water bottle at least once. Uber has managed to double-dip in predatory pricing, with several lawsuits allegedly saying they both: offered above-market incentive payments to drivers while offering below-market fares to passengers. While this put the company into a massive amount of debt (which they are still in), it didn't stop venture capital funds from throwing more money at them. At the same time, Uber was able to undercut any competition with other ride-sharing services (e.g., Lyft, Via) as well as the established taxicab companies with their stupid unions.

Uber even went a step further by launching clandestine campaigns against their competitors that included requesting rides on competitor's platforms and cancelling before the driver came, costing the other company money, or having Uber representatives poach drivers after requesting a ride. These projects had super-secret names like "Project Hell" and "SLOG." A final tactic that they have used is "surge pricing" to set higher prices during heightened demand. This coincides with the company using unusually low prices to undercut the competition during lower demand, thus taking consumers away from competitors. Because, come on, who wants more than one ride-sharing app on their phone? You need that space for all your other pointless apps and 1000s of pictures for your Instagram profile that gets 14 views. Uber understands your priorities.

You Got To Pay the Patent Troll

The term "Patent Troll" has a long history, dating all the way back to the ancient times known as the 1990s. It refers to the old Norwegian folktales of trolls, who exact tolls from travelers passing over bridges. Although he came before the actual term was popular, George Seldon is often considered one of the first patent trolls. He actually has a patent on the term "patent troll." George lived during those heady times of the late 1800s and early 1900s when oil-based cars were beginning to overtake the horse and carriage model. Seldon would end up suing Henry Ford (famed Nazi sympathizer) for a patent on the automobile that he had secured in the 1890s. The thing is, he never built or designed a working automobile. So, like any good aspiring oligarch, he looked to shortcut and steal the hard work of others.

He was successful for a couple of decades before Henry Ford (famed Nazi sympathizer) won an appeal in 1911. Despite this defeat and a failure to make anything better than some shitty truck company, Seldon still claimed a few hundred thousand dollars in royalties for doing nothing other than claiming a patent. Now think of what you could do with your bankroll and the litigious world of today. That's right, you can sue the literal pants off anyone and everyone.

The Trolls Of Today

The modern world has seen a major uptick in George Seldons in the technology industry. These trolls or Non-Practicing Entities (NPE) as they are called today get most of their money from licensing patents rather than creating anything of substance. And that is truly what an oligarch is all about.

These new age trolls collect patents like they are Pokémon cards. From a litigation perspective, some of the fiercest NPEs have more than 1,000 patents that hang over any technology company or startup that even thinks of trying to innovate an industry or provide a useful service. Sure, those companies can do that, they just have to pay the troll toll beforehand. After all, why should others benefit from these innovations if you don't get any money for being there first.

Some of the biggest patent troll companies are even sponsored by the top-tier technology giants as a way to crush any competition from startups or "disruptors" while remaining 1-2 degrees separated. Rockstar Consortium LLC, which owns nearly 3,500 patents is sponsored by Apple and Microsoft. It's main goal is to ensure that no company even has a whiff of innovation that can eat into their market share. Even Rockstar Games, the company that makes its money on promoting games about killing has a bit more moral fortitude. But who cares, you certainly shouldn't. You earned those patents. Well, you didn't earn them, but you own them. And owning is all that matters in the patent troll game of life.

The biggest patent troll of today and likely of all time is a company by the totally inconspicuous name of "Intellectual Ventures," which has a reported 60,000 – 70,000 patents. It was started by two former Microsoft stooges in 2000 and there is very little known about the company other than its litigiousness and patent arsenal. What is more intellectual than having so many patents that you ensure no one else can be intellectual in any industry at all? They call themselves a "global invention and investment business that creates, incubates, and commercializes inventions." That is code for we ensure we get fucking paid for any idea about anything that could make even a few cents. In fact, probably by the end of this paragraph, Intellectual Ventures will sue the author for using words like "innovation." Oh well, it was good while it lasted.

Some companies now partake in "defense patenting." This is where they buy up portfolios of patents (from many different companies) to protect themselves from someone trying to sue them. Google did this when they bought Motorola to avoid any lawsuits that may claim some of their Android phone technology was

Fig. 22: Trolls Love Patents, But They Hate Pants

stolen. Now, companies are just buying patents back and forth, because after all, that is far easier than actually creating new products and encouraging competition.

In any case, you can carry on with your own patent trolling of whatever industry you choose, or pick a few, life is short. So, be sure to utilize your life to ensure that others cannot innovate or improve businesses, themselves, society, or the short, pathetic lives of others.

Tipping the Scales

Now for another fun lesson about a boring topic. It is a nonstop thrill ride here and the next stop is Economies of Scale. Rather than getting into any in-depth details – go ask your economist friend if they haven't killed themselves yet – you will get the quick and dirty overview and why it can help you crush others by first helping the customers.

Helping the customers? Sounds counterintuitive to this book, but you will see why it can be beneficial. In the simplest of terms, Economies of Scale is when a company – typically a large one like you should have at this point – can reduce the prices of its goods because it can save production costs. In even simpler terms, this is why that box of Kraft Macaroni and Cheese that you eat over the sink alone at night costs only a dollar at Walmart, while the Mom-and-Pop store down the street has to sell it for double that price. You know the small store right? The one with the middle-aged cashier with the lazy eye that might be cute in the right light and might be winking at you or having a mild seizure. That one store cannot compete because of Economies of Scale.

In this way, you want to realize your Economy of Scale as quickly as possible. You can use this advantage to price out the competition, especially that Mom-and-Pop store with the cashier. Maybe you can hire her at your place and then she will finally say yes to your advances (she won't).

Economies of Scale have the added advantage of often contributing to a drop in employee morale over time because of the increased demand and need for more output. You can work your employees to death! Or at least to a severe alcohol problem. Plus, you can sell them alcohol at your mega stores. Either way, everyone wins, and the scales are balanced in life. By balanced of course meaning balanced completely toward benefitting you.

Favor Is Your Favorite Flavor

As discussed in Chapter 6, you should by now have a fair number of strings that you can pull to control various politicians and judges. This is where it can pay off handsomely by pulling these strings to strangle your competition. These strings usually manifest as laws or regulations. Say what? Aren't those exactly what you don't want? Yes and no.

Laws For Thee, Not For Me

There are several instances where it actually is beneficial for your giant conglomerate if Big Government passes laws and regulations. For instance, in the past several years, there has been a clamoring for higher hourly wages. A whole $15 an hour, which adjusted for inflation today comes to around $.03 and a handful of unsalted cashews. The state and federal laws that have been pushed to make $15 an hour were championed by some of the largest corporations in the world – Amazon, Walmart, and Costco. Seems counterintuitive, but it is actually brilliant. These companies can afford to invest in robots and Artificial Intelligence (AI) to replace their lowly wage slaves. Their competition of smaller and medium-sized businesses cannot afford it. Thus, the titans can force the guppies to pay their employees more and they can cut costs with more machines. Plus, the machines don't need wages, benefits, or cashews. To be fair, the employees don't need those things either.

It's Gonna Get Testy

In 2007, Mattel, one of the largest producers of children's toys, was forced to recall nearly 100,000 of them that contained lead paint. Exposure to lead has been proven to cause such ailments as intellectual disabilities, degradation of the nervous system, behavioral disorders, and a sudden desire to watch CNN. To be fair, CNN does go well with paint chips.

Mattel was forced to pay $2.3 million in civil lawsuits. The silver (well, lead) lining here is that following this event, Mattel sent its lobbyists to Congress to push for all toymakers to conduct lead testing. Was this because they cared about the children? Of course not. If they had it their way, they would produce their Hot Wheels cars with more lead or depleted uranium shells. No, this forced their competition – many who were smaller businesses – to conduct expensive lead testing on all their products. The small businesses complained, so Congress exempted companies that made less than 7,500 toys a year – a paltry amount. Thus, small companies were effectively kept small, if they shipped even a few more toys, they were subject to these expensive tests. Talk about turning lead into gold for the big guys.

Don't Let Them Ketchup

Henry Heinz, the German immigrant, who founded one of the largest condiment companies in the world was also keen on preventing others from encroaching on his territory. He drew a red, tomato-based line in the sand. In the early 20th century, he launched a campaign against the preservative, sodium benzoate. By this time, Heinz had removed sodium benzoate from his product, passing the 2-3 times increased cost to the consumer. His competitors, meanwhile, continued to use it in their products as it helped to keep costs down. Heinz managed to get Teddy Roosevelt in his corner to fight for the ban of sodium benzoate. While no law was passed, Heinz's campaign turned public opinion on the preservative and wiped out the competition. Despite scientists determining in 1908 that sodium benzoate was harmless, the damage had been done, and Heinz has dominated the market ever since. Who knows what dips that fries could have had if things had been different. One can dream.

As you can see, you have a host of options that you can mix and match to defeat your peers and stifle your competition. The longer you remain on top of your industry, the easier it becomes to ensure no one else even comes close to your rung of the ladder. You must be vigilant, as unfortunately there will likely be some enterprising jerk trying to disrupt or innovate in your field. The strategies mentioned above will allow you to snuff out any of these innovations before they have a chance to help humanity and hurt your wallet. Speaking of your wallet, in the next chapter, you will learn how to spread your cash and hide it across the world.

*Not just a
blank page!*

This almost
entirely
white space
is proudly
sponsored by the
activity of hiking
in Birkenstocks

CHAPTER 8

HIDING YOUR WEALTH

"Money often costs too much."

— RALPH WALDO EMERSON, POET, AND
HARD-TO-FIND PUZZLE CHARACTER

B y now you have accomplished a great many things, you've nearly reached the top of the oligarchy food chain. You have monopolized an industry, destroyed the working class, bought yourself a government, and crushed your peers and potential peers into submission. Now, what do you do with all your money? Hide it of course! There is always the dastardly taxman trying to get you to pay your fair share for the rest of society. You cannot let him have it – or anyone else for that matter. Let's take a look at all the wonderful ways in which you can avoid giving up even a single cent of your hard-earned, undeserved wealth.

LOOP DE LOOP

Before you look for those monetary hiding places around the world, you can first start with simply finding the open spaces in your country's tax laws. Almost all big corporations and billionaires do it, so it is perfectly normal and even better, it is legal.

Taxes are a funny thing, especially in the United States. Did you know that the Internal Revenue Service (IRS) actually knows how much you owe them each year? That's right. Filing your taxes is just a way for bored government bureaucrats to test whether you know how much you owe.

Most industrialized countries' governments simply send their citizens a letter saying how much they owe; the citizens pay and that is it. But where is the fun in that? Why not make the poor and middle class have to agonize over whether they kept all their receipts from the past year. Or make them grind their teeth over whether they should have filed form 1090EZ or 9576B12G? Do they qualify as a small business that operates on water, and what do they consider "water?" Is the water moving? Well then you'll need form WFT8895B unless that river has a dam, then its WFT8895BY5. They can always use TurboTax (who lobbied Congress to ensure that average Joe Public had to do this shit themselves) or H&R Block to determine how much they owe the IRS. Don't worry, you should already have an accounting team that does this all for you. Even better, they won't worry about forms because you won't be paying any taxes at all!

AVOID AT NO COST

Tax avoidance is one fairly straightforward, exploitative way to ensure you pay no tax. It is right there in the name, just avoid paying them. Easy. There are three methods that corporations utilize to make sure

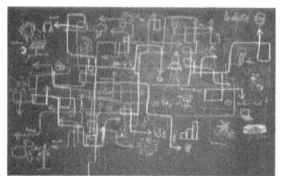

Fig. 23: The Novel Simplicity Of the United States Tax System

they can avoid paying any income tax. These methods cannot usually be used by individual citizens. First, a company can report operating losses for a year, meaning that they can literally say they made -$5 million last year and thus, don't owe the government anything. They can even carry this over for multiple years ensuring they give nothing back to the community. How, you ask?

Well, companies can deduct almost everything as part of their operation. Think factory costs, marketing, printing, hiring the mafia to break up unions, ice cream parties, you name it. They then remove these costs from their revenue and now they are at a loss. Ignore the fact that they have increased their foothold in the industry, bought up a few startups, and increased prices on goods. That's just part of operating a successful business.

APPRECIATE THE DEPRECIATION

Big corporations, like yourself, should – and do – buy up smaller assets like startups as they acquire more of a market. Guess what, you can write that off too! It's called "Accelerated Depreciation" and it means the government will let your corporation slide on the next few tax years because hell, you are growing the business and the economy (or so they would believe). You deserve a break for that work. Former mango president, Donald Trump, enacted the law that allowed these breaks in 2017.

CREDIT WHERE CREDIT ISN'T DUE

Finally, corporations love their credits. Whether it is carbon credits for doing fuck all, game credits at the local arcade, or in this case, tax credits. For instance, a company can deduct half a million dollars in tax if they invested that money into Research & Development (R&D) in the previous year. In 2022, this cost the government over $20 billion in collected taxes. The kicker? There is not a whole lot of official legal government language on exactly what constitutes legitimate R&D. So, you can potentially have your textile conglomerate put $500 million into researching whether or not that Chartreuse polo shirt looks good on you. It probably doesn't, but those scientists and engineers will give you the thumbs up. It's on the government's dime anyway.

Give Back To Get Back

This somewhat overlaps tax avoidance but is worth mentioning separately here. Philanthropy has become a tried-and-true method for billionaires to pretend to care about the poor children with aids, or the poor aides with children, or whatever the hell you want. There are countless foundations that billionaires and multi-millionaires have set up and even more stories about the wealthy donating obscene amounts of money to a charitable cause.

Don't be fooled, they don't give a shit about any of these people or the associated causes. Why do they do it then? It's a huge tax write-off. Or even better, they donate huge swaths of cash to their own charity. For instance, Elon Musk gave $4 million in 2022 to the "Future of Life Institute," which focuses on reducing the risks of AI and biotechnology. Let's ignore the fact that $4 million to Elon Musk is the equivalent of a Zimbabwean dollar to the King of England. The charity is actually owned by Musk, so effectively, he donated money to himself. Sure, some of it will probably go to the actual charity and its work, but he can now write that money off and look like a decent person in the process. It is a win-win for Elmo. He did a similar act by donating Tesla shares valued at $5.7 million to the little-known charity, the "Musk Foundation." No one is quite sure who owns that charity as of today.

Nicolas Woodman, the billionaire founder of GoPro and human equivalent of a warm Red Bull, pulled over a similar stunt when he "donated" 500 million shares to his own foundation: the Jill and Nicolas Woodman Foundation (no accounting for originality with the billionaire class). He immediately received a tax write-off for it in 2014. Four years later, the New York Times reported that the foundation had received none of the donation amount. Instead, the money sat in a Silicon Valley Community Foundation (i.e., an account in Silicon Valley), which is not required to disclose any information about donors or activity. It even allows you to utilize it as a glorified checking account. You get all the benefits of a checking account plus tax benefits and none of the accountability. This obviously means that it is totally above level. If only someone had some sort of device to record what was going on. The world may never know.

Come Out Of Your Shell

Before you look beyond your borders to see what wonderful investment opportunities await you, first you need to create a shell company. These companies are the standard that the oligarch class uses to move their money, hide their money, and invest their money without the need to pay any fees to mettlesome governments and nosy tax authorities.

In the simplest of terms, a shell company is one that operates without any business operations or assets. Say you decided to start a corporation. Let's call it "Ireland & Overseas Acquisitions and Milton Corporate Services." Then you decide to not acquire anything, rent out any office space, provide any services, or create any products. All you do is have a bank account and maybe a P.O. Box for your company. Ta Da! You have a shell company. Now, you can funnel your money into it, and from there, well, there is no telling where or what you can do with that money. No, really. There really isn't any way to tell by most authorities.

From here, you can get more creative as you incorporate more shell companies in different tax havens. You can utilize this network of companies to constantly move money around, whether it is from legal or illegal means. Even if the authorities catch on to what you may be doing and think you may not be paying your fair share at home, it'll take teams of forensic tax professionals years to follow the trail with no guarantee they will ever find the end. It is like the fable of the Tortoise and the Hare, except the Tortoise has unlimited funds, isn't bound by the racetrack, and also is paying off friends of the Hare to keep him behind.

With that in mind, you now should be quickly coming up with a few shell companies, names, and picking out what countries you want to incorporate them in for your purposes. But first, let's take a brief look at the concept of keeping your money out of your country.

TAKE TO THE SEA

In the Disney movie, *The Little Mermaid*, when Sebastian the crab sings "Under the Sea," it is clear he is telling Ariel to invest her hard-earned shells and kelp in offshore accounts. Don't bother looking that up, just assume it is true.

As you start making your millions and then billions, you will want to begin moving it to various oceanic tax havens located around the world. Sure, it's fun to exploit the tax loopholes on land in your country, but why not let your money take a tropical vacation? It has been working hard all these years after all.

Known as "Offshore Banking," this tactic has been used by oligarchs and oligarchs-lite for decades. It is a rather mundane undertaking as you will be using your army of accountants and lawyers to take the money you earned in your home country and moving it to an offshore bank (note, it may not always be adjacent to a body of water) to gain interest while avoiding any pesky capital gains taxes (i.e., taxes on investment profits). This is often done with the use of a shell company, which you should now know how to create for any purpose.

Fig. 24: "Take It From Me. Every Bank Is Better Out In The Sea"

Offshore banking was originally conceived as a way for wealthy individuals to keep their money safe if they lived in a country that was politically unstable. Unstable countries subject to coups would often lead to banks and wealthy assets being seized by the incoming party (i.e., the poorer party). Thus, offshore banking is not inherently illegal. In fact, all of these tactics that oligarchs use only ever wade into the "grey area" of international law. That's why you rarely see anyone prosecuted or any funds taken except for the most egregious users and the worst of people, like war criminals, the mafia, or whoever invented black licorice candy. Each deserve a swift trial at The Hague.

So, where can you take advantage of these high-interest, zero-tax accounts for your wealth? Let's take a look at some options.

- Seychelles: This is the smallest African country and is located in the Somali Sea, in the Northwest of the Indian Ocean. You may have heard the name before as it is famous for being used by the leader of the mercenary group, Blackwater, Erik Prince, to establish a backchannel between the Trump administration and Vladimir Putin. But, it has so much more than just mild treason going for it! It is also a major haven for the wealthy elite, especially the political elite, to stash their cash with no questions asked. There are hundreds of shell companies based out of here, many are used as a medium to send money through as it is moved to other shell companies around the world to avoid any paper trail. Seychelles maintains policies that protect the identities of these shell companies making it easy to conduct clandestine business through this tiny island. Unless of course you are Trump, then the whole world finds out rather quickly.

- Cayman Islands: You have no doubt heard about this tax haven. It is by far one of the most popular of them all. This luxury resort island requires virtually no taxes at all and has some of the laxest reporting laws in the world. It is too hot after all to be sitting inside all day poring over spreadsheets, better to take the oligarch's word for it and get some sun and a refreshing Pina Colada instead.

- Cyprus: This small island south of Greece in the Mediterranean Sea has been the subject of plenty of scandals in the past few years. In 2019, it was caught selling EU citizenship for $2 million to any foreign investor that felt like having an extra passport. This is also known as a "Golden Passport." Cyprus is a favorite money mainstay for the Russian oligarchs of today. Before the start of the Ukraine war in 2022, this island of pristine beaches was frequented by Russian millionaires and billionaires to vacation or park their super yachts. Since the war started, well, it still has been a place to park their super yachts, but also their super bank accounts. Despite massive international sanctions led by the United States, Cyprus has had no qualms about storing and hiding the extreme wealth of the Russian oligarchs. As clear as the water is by the beaches, Cyprus's banking is more opaque than ever. When questioned, the Cypriot finance minister in 2023 said that these accounts were under "increased scrutiny," which by Cypriot standards means they are likely going to do fuck all. So, if your empire is attached to any international criminal organization, and more than likely, it will be at some point, then take a super yacht down to the shores of Limassol and maybe grab a golden passport while you are there. You never can have too many different passports.

- Singapore: Once the crown jewel of Britain in the East, Singapore has become a haven for the rich in storing their own crown jewels, an estimated $470 billion as of 2018. The new oligarchs of China have made this a major center to deposit their funds in an attempt to avoid Emperor Pooh from stealing their money on the Chinese mainland. Singapore's stability in terms of politics and economics adds a glimmering allure to the country for your offshore needs. While it may be illegal to chew gum (well, partly), it certainly isn't illegal to hide your wealth here with little to no tax and fear of your accounts being found or seized. An added bonus if you use Singapore for one of your offshore havens is that it is one of the top banking centers in Asia – even the world – so you will have no shortage of financial investment advice for your accounts. Go ahead and chew your gum there, you earned it. *Double Your Pleasure, Double Your Fund.*

- Samoa: Looking for an alternative to the Caribbean and American Virgin Islands for your offshore accounts? Tired of having to share your legal gray areas with the new rich? Well, look no further than the island nation of Samoa. No, not American Samoa. The other one. Popular for providing some of the best – or at least biggest – rugby players in the world, this small Polynesian country in the Pacific also hosts very large accounts of the richest people and companies in the world. In Samoa, corporations do not need to maintain accounting records or register any names or identities of their shareholders with the authorities. It is hard to blame Samoa for hosting the oligarchs of the world, they are tiny compared to some of the other countries that participate in offshore hosting. Still, it means they are more than happy to help you out, so why not give them a try? Perhaps you will even figure out how in the hell to play rugby.

- Switzerland: While not technically at sea, or even near a large body of water, you cannot talk about hidden bank accounts without mentioning the grandfather of it all, the Swiss. Although investments in the neutral state have fallen considerably since 2010 when the U.S. Department of Justice forced the banks to open up their records. The Swiss can still hide with the big boys, so do not underestimate them.

- This bullet is sponsored by *Big Tony's All-Age, All-American Bullet Shop: "We're gunning for you, kid!"*

In 1934, Switzerland formalized their banking laws to make it a criminal offense to reveal the name of any account holders. Under this and other Swiss laws, bankers act much like doctors or lawyers in patient/client confidentiality. If you have herpes and are laundering money, no one will ever know if you are operating out of Switzerland.

Switzerland has a long and storied history in storing money for the richest and worst of humanity. When it came to war, Switzerland remained neutral in fighting, but was always happy to help warmongers on both sides conduct banking. After all, war is profitable (more on that in Chapter 10).

And profit the Swiss did. It is well documented that Swiss bankers kept Nazi gold during WWII and beyond. In 1998, a Swiss commission estimated that $440 million of Nazi gold was looted and stored in the country during the war. That is nearly $8 billion in today's currency.

Thankfully today, Switzerland has finally moved on from the Nazis...and right into the arms of the Russian oligarchs. It is estimated that across all of the Swiss banks, over $8 billion from the Russian central bank is being stored. After plenty of pressure from the European Union (EU), the country froze the assets and reserves from the Russian central bank. For now.

While the small islands dominate the offshore bank account world, there is still some prestige in storing a few hundred million in the vaults of Geneva and Zurich. James Bond uses it for his banking after all, and who wouldn't want to be that cool? If you pay enough, you might be able to name the next movie even.

Perhaps, *Carte Blanche* (actual Ian Fleming novel), or "You Only Deposit Twice," or even "The Banker Who Loved Me."

Pandora's Golden Box

It was James Cameron that first discovered the offshore accounts of the rich and famous. Wait, no he did that movie about blue people. No, it was a number of brave journalists that released what is now known as the Pandora Papers. A trove of documents that has shown how some of the most rich and famous have used the tactics and countries described in the previous section to hide their wealth from Mr. Tax Man. Let's take a look at some of the big names that have blazed the path of offshore accounting, but stupidly got caught by the media. Even the Na'vi were better at hiding. Take 90 percent of the lessons from these people, just like you would take 90 percent of your employees' salary.

- Abdullah II, King of Jordan: A well-liked ruler in the Middle East and one of the few who doesn't resort to killing anyone who jaywalks. The King since 1999, Abdullah II has been a friend to the West and most countries. Still, a King has got to get paid. And King Abdullah II funneled nearly $100 million through secret (i.e., shell companies) to buy luxury homes across the world. He used accounts in Switzerland and the Caribbean to carry out most of these trades. Look, he is a king. He needs 14 luxury homes – which are listed in the United Kingdom and the United States, the third world of the West these days. One posh home in particular was bought in Los Angeles. It is a 7-bedroom (meh, kind of small), that overlooks the Pacific Ocean and towards his secret offshore accounts thousands of miles west.

- Tony Blair, Former Prime Minister of the United Kingdom: Sir Anthony Charles Lynton Blair KG (yes, that is his official name) led the now defunct country of the United Kingdom (UK) from 1997 – 2007. After his reign of mediocrity, he and his wife decided to buy a simple property for nearly 7 million pounds. They bought it from an offshore company, but the Blairs insisted it was under UK control. Of course, they have no reason not to be believed so that is the end of that. Except that Mr. Blair had some dealings with the mortgage of the property and they managed to avoid 350 thousand pounds (whatever that is in freedom dollars) in taxes. The Blairs now have nearly 40 properties worth north of 35 million pounds since he left office. Brexit may have happened, but it certainly didn't affect the Blairs. They aren't immigrants after all.

- <u>Shakira, Queen of Belly Dancing:</u> Her hips may not lie, but her accounts and her wallet sure as hell do. Ms. Ripoli (her real name), managed to skirt over $15 million in taxes utilizing shell companies as tax havens. Wherever, whenever she wanted, she had a place to put her money from the profits of that song. She may face a whopping $24 million fine for her transgressions. Oh no. She may have to shake a few extra times to get that money out. Maybe she can Waka Waka a few more bucks out of Africa.

- <u>Juan Carlos I, Former King of Spain:</u> The Pandora Papers have labeled over 600 Spaniards as being part of illegal, offshore accounting. Sadly, when you are king, everyone looks at you first. Nothing is fair when you are ultra rich. Former King Carlos, who sadly abdicated to democracy in 2014, has been named in these papers where he was due to receive nearly 30 percent of a deal from a Danish private fund. For what, you ask? The hell if anyone knows. The fact that a former King needs a bit more cash says a lot.

He probably spent it on tapas. Have you seen how expensive those tiny plates are? Ridiculous.

- <u>Pep Guardiola, Premier of the Premier League:</u> While we're on the Iberian peninsula, Pep managed to secure at least 500 million euros through a bank account in Andorra (a tiny little haven between France and Spain) without tax. Not a bad take considering he makes more coaching a top tier team in the English Football Premier League. But look, you always need more money. It may be prudent for you to buy a football team and a similar Pep to guide it to winning. The Middle East now dominates ownership in the English Premier League, so you will have to compete with the entire public funds of these countries, but Russian oligarchs like Roman Abramovich (former owner of the Premier League Football Club, Chelsea) did alright before the Ukraine-Russia war, so there is no reason you can't do as well or better. War and Football, that's all that you need to pay for to have some fun with your oligarch money. And if you do it right, you'll end up making more money on both than what you initially put in. A great investment whether it is about providing balls or bombs.

- <u>Elton John, King of the Yellow Brick Road:</u> A little runt that was raised in the suburbs of London, Reginald Dwight (seriously, no one uses their real name), is one of the greatest original artists of the last few decades. Sure, he loved lots of drugs and sex, but did you know he hated taxes? He may have been too drugged out to know what his accountants were doing, but it certainly helped him escape a bit of taxes, a few hundred thousand pounds worth to be sure. Anything he owed might has well have been a candle in the wind.

- Ringo Starr, Some Random Drummer: He was once a part of a niche band in the 1960s called "The Beatles." No one has heard of that band since then. Sir Richard Starkey (yes, that is his real name), managed to make a great name for himself in the decades following the band's dissolution. Ringo set up a P.O. Box company in various tax havens, including the British Virgin Islands, Panama, and the Bahamas. He tried his hardest to invest all his money in himself, but it turns out he needed a little help from his friends. In this case, his friends were accountants and illegal investors in the Caribbean. Ah well, the tax man will likely let it be.

A Man, A Plan, Some Wealth, Panama

Before there was Pandora, there was the Panama Papers. This scandal included a leak of over 11 million confidential documents from a Panamanian law firm. If you don't know already, Panama allows most people to declare themselves citizens on a few light requirements. Incidentally, it is a paradise for the rich and the richer. These OG papers provided a clear look into the shell companies that various corporations, rich assholes, and the celebrity elite utilize. Some of these famous people include:

- Gianni Infantino, President of FIFA: He is gay, he is an immigrant, he is black, he is white, he is green, he is poor, he is a worker, he understands everyone. This is paraphrased from his bizarre speech during the winter World Cup of 2022. Is it any surprise that this Swiss-Italian, bald douche doesn't pay his taxes? No. The answer is a definitive no.

- Lionel Messi, Argentine Footballer: One of the best football players to ever grace the pitch, his $100 million plus a year wasn't enough for the former La

Liga player. He had to ensure that he didn't pay a
Euro cent. In fact, he scored more goals and assists
than he paid in euro dollars.

- Jackie Chan, Rush Hour Detective: The Hong Kong
  action star and Chinese Communist party (CCP)
  darling had to unfortunately keep his money away
  from Chris Tucker and others. Tax officials tried to
  look into his records, but they ended up getting a few
  kicks to their face instead.

- Emma Watson, Hermione: One of the child stars of
  the Harry Potter franchise decided she needed to hide
  some of those galleons outside of Gringotts bank and
  in the British Virgin Islands. She has managed to
  avoid most media attention from the papers despite
  this. Expelliarmus Taxus!

- Mormon Church, Salt Lake Sect: Yes, these Desert
  derelicts did avoid taxes on nearly $30 million in
  profits. Will they admit it? Of course not, in fact, all
  the internet searches will lead to Mormon-based
  newspapers claiming this is a lie. It is up to you to
  determine if the always faithful Latter-Day Saints
  Church (LDS) is totally telling the truth about
  money. The Church was founded on complete truth
  by Joseph Smith after all. Why would they lie?
  Because they want to avoid any taxes and build more
  churches or buy more government land in Utah? No,
  that cannot be the reason.

A Whale Of A Time

Meet Jho Low. Jho Low is from Malaysia and is one of the richest
and most prolific abusers of offshore accounting ever to exist. So,
you may want to read this section carefully so you can learn from
a master.

Mr. Low is the key figure in the 1Malaysia Development Berhad (1MDB) scandal. This scandal involved the embezzling of over $700 million from the Malaysian government's public investment fund (i.e., a fund for improving infrastructure and other societal aspects in the country).

Jho Low took this money and funneled it through several shell companies and countries, going back and forth, forth, and back, between them to ensure the trail was nearly impossible to follow. He used this illegal cash to pay for all sorts of luxuries, including a superyacht, the Equanimity, luxury homes and properties across every continent, and in the most famous acquisition, a movie studio. This movie studio, Red Granite Pictures, would fund several movies, most famously, *The Wolf of Wall Street*, a movie about a rich investment banker that screwed over everyone who invested with him, played by Leonardo DiCaprio.

Fig. 25: Jho Low Seen Here With A Random Fan

This Ponzi scheme rivals that of Bernie Madoff. Mr. Low aimed to scheme an additional $5 billion from the Malaysian investment fund before he was caught. He eventually entered into a settlement in 2019 with the U.S. government to avoid any court proceedings across his civil, criminal, and administrative cases against him. In that same year, he was accused of yet another laundering scheme, this time with the famous Korean rapper, PSY. Although all charges were dismissed due to lack of evidence, the stink of the affair was definitely not the style of the Gangnam area of South Korea. Two years later, he was accused of illegal lobbying in China. Despite all his egregious crimes, Jho Low has managed to escape with barely a slap on the wrist. It was the politician, Najib Razak, that had to face charges of the stolen money. This is a prime example for you. You can basically get away with anything if you hide your money across offshore accounts, even if it is in the billions.

If a fat, 30-something movie entrepreneur can do it, so can you. Now, you may not have the resources of an entire country's investment fund, unless you are coming from a Middle Eastern or Southeast Asian country, you still should be able to utilize your multi-millions or billions to conduct similar actions and get away with them. Maybe you can even get Leonardo DiCaprio to act in a specific role for you.

A Bank By Any Other Name

Deutsche Bank, the German multinational investment bank and financial services company, is based in Frankfurt, Germany. It was founded in the 1870s and has done its best to help the most crooked of companies and people in the 100+ years since then. It isn't a criminal enterprise; it is a criminal tradition. Make sure you have that right. It is difficult to focus on just one scandal Deutsche Bank has been a part of, so let's look at a just a few in the last decade.

The LIBOR scandal was a scheme where bankers across financial institutions colluded to manipulate the interest rate in which banks loan each other money. Basically, these banks, led by Deutsche, decided, "hey, let's just not charge each other a whole lot of money and we can share money to invest in things that no one else knows of in the world." Deutsche isn't alone in this case, Barclays Bank, Citigroup, and JPMorgan were among the others that participated in this illegal rate exchange.

Deutsche Bank may be most famous for providing large, incredible loans to Donald Trump. For over 10 years, Deutsche Bank has loaned money to Trump, despite his lack of paying anyone for anything, ever. That is excellent due diligence by Deutsche. Which means, they are a great bank to utilize for yourself. You can take out massive loans from them, use this money to buy whatever you want, and never pay the bank back. Trump never has, why should you? The bank will figure it out in the end, and they will likely get the government to bail them out because they are too big to fail anyway.

Trump managed to get his money from this reckless bank by exaggerating the value of this properties, including the cardboard box that is Trump Towers in Manhattan. He was able to pass off faulty records as true and the great MBA business minds at Deutsche just nodded their heads in acceptance.

Besides the Orange Cheeto, Deutsche has also made a name for itself in violating U.S. sanctions against Iran, Libya, Syria, Burma, and Sudan. They couldn't have possibly stuck to these sanctions after all. There was nearly $11 billion at stake. Why won't the U.S. government think of the profit margins?

Outside of Switzerland, Deutsche Bank has been one of the biggest supporters of Russian money-laundering with over $10 billion being laundered out of Russia in the last six years. International investigations discovered that this work may have involved as much as $80 billion in Russian oligarch money being moved out of the country and into shell companies.

Even after the beginning of the Ukraine – Russia war in 2022, Deutsche Bank refused to shut down its support of its Russian clients despite sanctions. Yes, people were dying, but has anyone thought of the poor shareholders and Vice Presidents at Deutsche? No, they didn't, those monsters. Deutsche Bank continues to be a great avenue for funneling your funds into the vast network of shell companies and tropical islands. You can't be a rich douche without Deutsche.

Home Sour Home

Fig. 26: 2 Bedroom Home, Good Location, White Picket Fence, $625,000

Back before the 1980s, buying a house was nothing more than a simple rite of passage. If you had a GED (hell, if you didn't), and a minimum wage job, you could afford a 2 or 3-bedroom home, a white picket fence, a white picket wife, a white picket child or two, and a white picket car. There is nothing like being able to afford the American dream with a cashier job at Wendy's. Now, you'll be lucky to be able to afford a rental in the dumpster behind Wendy's.

Not you though. Those worries are for the poors, the newly indentured serfs, the fast-food slaves. For you, housing is a game of numbers and a game of hiding. By this point, you should have at least 3 or 4 places around the world. Yes, they are often for vacation or to visit your mistress, but they can be so much more. In this case, they can be for hiding money from the Tax Man.

Russian and Chinese oligarchs are experts in the housing game. Do you know why housing prices in your liberal city, whether it be in the United States or Canada, or Western Europe, are so expensive? Well, friend, it is because billionaires from Russia and China are buying up entire pieces of land or apartment buildings. They are doing this because they can utilize these purchases as investments that won't be seized or taxed by their governments.

There are entire apartment buildings in cities like Vancouver, Toronto, New York City, and San Francisco that have no renters, no people living in them, and no advertisements to rent or buy. Thus, the prices of places where the actual locals want to live or rent go up in price due to the exorbitant amount that is paid for these properties around them.

These real estate properties are also used for laundering money. The governments of these countries can do very little to discover who is buying and moving money through these properties. Since late 2018, more than $2.3 billion has been laundered through U.S. real estate alone. That is not to mention the money that flows through art, jewelry, and luxury craft (e.g., yachts). This is perfect for you as you will have no one looking over your shoulder as you buy up properties around the Western world, not to mention plenty of places in even less regulated areas of the globe.

While legislation has been approved in the U.S. and Canada to prevent tax evaders through real estate, there is no real "teeth" to the law. This means you can continue to do what you want, the worst that will happen is you'll get caught, wait five years for a conviction and pay 1/20 of the change in your pocket for violating the law. Remember, any law with a fine means that it is legal for you, and illegal for anyone poor. So, don't feel guilty about watching House Hunters on HGTV, or for flipping through that real estate magazine. You deserve it. Think of all those homes as just fancy bank accounts with Corinthian Columns. The columns are tax deductible too.

Congratulations! Your money should now be well hidden from everyone. It is no longer just in that ditch in your mother's backyard where you buried all the bodies of your competition; that should now be separate. No, you have done the work, established the shell companies, and moved that beautiful money of yours across the longitudes and latitudes of the world so no one can find it but you and maybe one accountant.

You have now ensured that the majority of the wealth you took from your country and its people will not be taken back or taken by others. It is yours forever, not even your awful spawn can get it without you dying and leaving intricate clues for them to find where it is in the world. It's like the Carmen San Diego of illegal funds.

Unfortunately, while you can hide all this money, the miserable poor are becoming restless. They will never know where you keep your funds, but they will know they aren't being kept in the country. Thanks democrats for your stupid transparency laws. The next chapter will discuss how you can keep these poor folks down, or at least sated and quiet as you continue to rape the world of its natural resources for your own gain. Let's take a look at how!

CHAPTER 9

THE REVOLTING REVOLTS

"When we hang capitalists,
   they will sell us the rope we use."

— JOSEPH STALIN, COMMUNIST GOOD BOY

They are coming. They are here. Yes, the clamor of the poor is becoming ever louder. Especially as you gain more wealth and leave less and less for the rest. This is not a new phenomenon. Unfortunately, the wretched poors have been a nuisance for a few thousand years. They know what they are doing, and so you should know how they work and how to stamp them out. Know thy enemy.

ALL PLEBS LEAD TO ROME

The "plebs" or the plebian class was the working class in Ancient Rome. They were basically one step above the slaves during that time. So, think of them as the middle class of today. Those who run the human resources of a small company, those who manage the local tire shop, those who aren't poor enough for food stamps but aren't rich enough to understand their 401k. Those are the plebs. "Secessio Plebs" is when these middle-class ghouls decided that enough was enough and stopped doing any work that was needed for Rome, like building roads or abusing the Gauls (Germans). This was the equivalent of a protest and shut down much of the Roman way of life. It was basically an early form of unionizing (more on that shortly) and the rich class of Rome and the Senate had to sadly kotow to their demands each time. Now, back then they tried to just throw a few hundred soldiers at the plebians, but even then, you have to worry about angering the majority of Roman citizens, so it wasn't used often by the rich. These days, unions are basically worthless thanks to the unadulterated growth of pure capitalism. Yet, some have found success and others have continued to hang on despite attempts by governments around the world trying to squash them at every turn.

UNIONS: UP YOURS, UPTON SINCLAIR

The modern form of unions were formed in the last 150 years. Many came to be after the publishing of "The Jungle" by Upton Sinclair. The book describes the horrid conditions of a meatpacking factory. Associations rose up to demand better working conditions from their seniors. These associations of workers thought they could take power over their overlords and managers. Unfortunately, some were successful.

Fig. 27: A Lighthearted Look At The Joys Of Meatpacking Factories, for Ages 3 and Up

In essence, a union is an association of greedy, low-level, and mid-level workers who collaborate to negotiate against their employer. These negotiations usually involve improving the working conditions of employees, increasing pay, or ensuring that employees have a certain set of rights. The absolute nerve of them.

The initial rise of these infernal unions began in the middle of the Industrial Revolution, which started in the mid-18th century and lasted through the early to mid-19th century. The Industrial Revolution brought many new innovations to the world, including the steam-powered locomotive, the cotton gin, cotton-flavored gin, and the electrical telegraph. Even better though, the revolution brought in a stream of poor, needy workers from the farmlands to work the vast numbers of machinery of the new era. What awaited these workers in their new urban utopia? Let's find out:

- State-of-the-Art Living Conditions: Much like the New York City housing market of today, factory workers lived in tiny, low-rise apartments, stacked poorly on top of one another and grossly overcrowded. The genius landlords of the time cut corners and used the finest quality of cheap materials to build these slums. You can still see similar slums today in places like: Chennai, India; Kiberia, Nairobi; and Trenton, New Jersey.

- Modern Workplaces: Finally, the farmers and rural workers of the time could spend their days in new, sleek industrial environments. For instance, in many of the new factories that had popped up, workers could be treated to an open concept space free from the clutter of safety regulations. Eventually, you could free yourself of some of those fingers and limbs during your time. Or, perhaps the mines would be more stylish, with constant cave-ins, gas explosions, and lung diseases. It is probably better than working at Twitter these days.

- Opportunities For Children: With new factories came new daycares for the little ones. Instead of wiling away the hours at school, the children were able to work the same dangerous jobs as their parents (if they had any that is), often even for longer and with little pay. It was just like an internship in corporate America, they were paid with experience. They should have been thankful just for the opportunity.

- A New Purpose: No purpose that is, but that is still new in a sense. Workers lost much of their personal autonomy that they were used to enjoying in the fields back home. They were able to shed those unnecessary things like pride, joy, and job satisfaction that were weighing them down in the pre-industrial days. Now, they were able to enjoy the utter pointlessness of life in the modern workforce. Sort of like working in an Amazon Fulfillment Center, but not quite that depressing.

Alas, someone always has to come and ruin the fun. And so, unions were formed. The first coming as early as the 1790s, with shoemakers in Philadelphia. Eventually, other unions were formed, made up of tailors, traders, and other artisans as they were swallowed up in the Industrial Revolution. A National Labor Movement would sadly create a shorter workday and a minimum wage. Workers were gaining rights. Once the union bottle was opened, it was difficult to close. But not impossible! Let's find out how you can break unions for yourself and take back the factory.

The Empire Strikes Back

It is time for you to stop those good-for-nothing unions from making you pay for workers' fair wages, or ensure their safety, or other benefits. The wonderful tradition of strikebreaking or union busting started not long after the rapid expansion of unions in the latter half of the 19th century and continues to this day.

So, let's look at some of the simple ways for how you can hire your own goon squad of thugs by learning how others did it before you.

A point of clarification. Despite its name, strikebreaking does often have a softer side. It can concern the hiring of "scabs," or people who will work in place of union employees who are on strike and refusing to work at a given time. Companies would hire agencies to provide them with these scabs to replace their ungrateful unionized workers. Thus, the customers are happy, and capitalism keeps on humming along. John D. Rockefeller was an active proponent of this in the 1870s with oil refinery workers. You may opt for this tactic if you are facing a smaller strike, maybe one full of nerds, like for example the Writer's Guild of America (WGA) strike of 2023. Although be careful, they might write jokes about you in a book or Netflix show some-day. The horror. For the bigger, badder unions, you may have to get your hands – meaning someone else's hands – a bit dirty.

Bust A Move

Well, you tried to hire a bunch of scabs to replace those union workers marching outside the gate with their posterboards. Turns out they were a bit tougher than they looked and you couldn't get the scabs into your factory. It's time to get physical. Union busting has a rich history involving the mob. In the early to mid-20th century, organized criminal groups such as La Cosa Nostra (i.e., Mafia) were able to make their way into labor unions through corruption, intimidation, and really cool hats. They would use these tactics to then instill fear among employers and members of the union to ensure they stayed in line. This was sometimes known as "Labor Racketeering," which is as sexy of a crime as it sounds.

One of the greatest examples of this type of work was that which was done by the Corporations Auxiliary Company, a name as ominous as it is uninteresting. This is probably why they operated under a dozen other names in the early decades of the 20th century. The company would send its employees into unions, have them elected to the board and often destroy the union through intimidation, corrupt payments, and overall sabotage. These spies would even work in the factories and offices, collecting information on employees. They also would lick all the donuts in the break room and never refill the coffee when it was finished. They were a menace. By the late 1930s, they had nearly 500 companies they were watching in some capacity across ten cities in the United States. Much of this work was often known as "Industrial Espionage," which is as sexy of a crime as it sounds.

Swing Low, Sweet Oligarch

Ludlow is now no more than an abandoned town in the foothills of Southern Colorado. Although, it somehow still has the best Tex Mex this side of the Sierra Nevada. Back in the early 20th century, though, it was a booming mining town. The Colorado Fuel and Iron Company (CFIC), owned by none other than John D. Rockefeller was the sole labor provider and owner of the mines and coke (no, sadly not that coke, or the drink, even more boring) ovens nearby.

In the early fall of 1913, these unappreciative workers and their families went on strikes for outrageous things like better wages and living conditions, and free vouchers for the nearby Tex Mex restaurant that had raised its prices. Rockefeller and his partner, Lamont Bowers, were angry that the increased wages for these workers had cut into their profit margin. It was due to be the most profitable earnings in the history of the company, but people needed to feed their families, the gall of them. So, the CFIC did what any company owned by reasonable rich people would do, they massacred the Ludlow mining camp. Local militia and the Colorado national guard killed 25 of the strikers, including 12 women and children. Thereby ending the mining camp's reign of terror on corporate profits.

Unfortunately, this was a century ago and it has become harder to simple murder union employees who are striking against your company. But who knows, with today's political climate and government ineptitude, you may soon be able to legally murder your employees again.

ONLY YOU CAN PREVENT LIVABLE WAGES

You don't necessarily have to resort to murder. Your loss, let the other oligarchs have all the fun. Maybe later. There are still ways you can stop unions from even getting to the point of striking. Let's look at a few tools at your disposal that can help nip any strikes in the bud.

SURVEY SAYS, IT'S THEIR FAULT

As discussed in an earlier chapter, public opinion is very useful. When it comes to stopping unions, or promoting capitalism, or murdering someone in the middle of 5th avenue, public opinion can make or break you. Thus, when it comes to prevention, you can follow in the footsteps of dictators. By turning the court of public opinion onto someone else instead of you, you can ensure that any union activity will not last long, if at all. That's right, friend, it is time for another round of "The Blame Game!" It is a bit different than the "Wheel of Blame" from the previous book, "So You Want To Be A Dictator." This time, a la Family Feud, you can choose the top five answers from a survey of 100 oligarchs and capitalists. Just as dictators utilize the "look over there" approach to hiding their misdeeds, you can also use it for the same purpose. Let's see the top answers on the board.

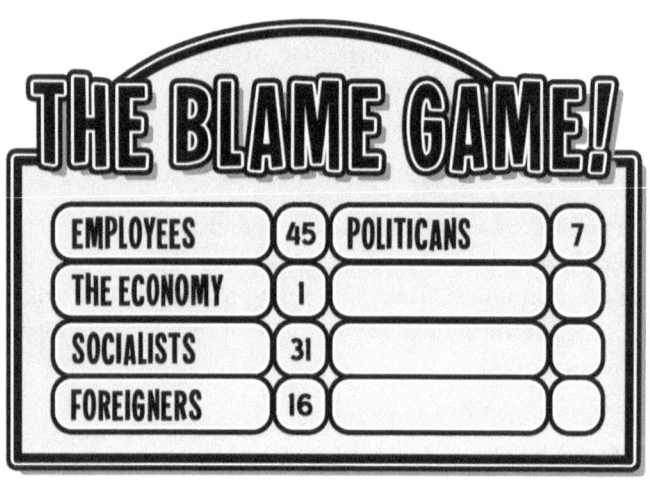

THE BLAME GAME!

EMPLOYEES	45	POLITICANS	7
THE ECONOMY	1		
SOCIALISTS	31		
FOREIGNERS	16		

SOCIALISTS: THE GREATEST EVIL

This is a fairly easy one and no wonder a majority of oligarchs chose it. As mentioned earlier, socialism was founded by a bunch of lazy people who thought everyone deserved the basic necessities in life. Today, you can use it to basically mean anything, and a majority of people will get angry about it. Here are a few things that have been called socialism by oligarchs and their political stooges:

- *Universal Healthcare* – No surprise here, why would you want to give everyone the opportunity to live? People need to pay to live.
- *Affordable Housing* – Get that shit out of here, people are fine in their tent cities. They don't need decent homes or social care. They would just spend it on socialist drugs, like crystal meth or heating in the winter.
- *Essential Infrastructure* – Yep, you can even call things like repairing bridges, filling potholes, or providing reliable, clean water as unnecessary and part of the "Nanny State."

Employees: No One Wants To Work Anymore

This has been a popular mantra from the richest class and business owners for a few years now, especially post-pandemic. However, the phrase actually originates from 1894 and can be seen in various articles throughout the 20th century as rich capitalists continue to complain about the ungrateful working class. It is still true today that no one wants to work. It's not because the prices of food, housing, healthcare, gas, and more have gone up exponentially in the last 30 years while wages have remained stagnant. No. It's not because workers are expected to work for pennies, with no benefits, and with no rights. No. It's because they are lazy and just want to sit at home, eat potato chips, smoke weed, and watch their favorite PBS Frontline documentary. Jokes on them, they only release a few of those a year.

Foreigners: Low-Hanging Fruit

A classic one that has been in use since time immemorial. This one actually has a bit of utility depending on the situation. Why are wages so low? "Well, it's because foreign interests are undercutting prices and causing us all to tighten belts. Except you of course, you'll get a bonus. Or, you can say that the union has been infiltrated by foreign agents trying to undermine the entire company.

Politicians: Easily Disposable

Once again, you can throw the blame squarely on the government. Of course, you can have one of your own paid off congresspeople do this for you and blame the other side. For instance, you can blame the one side for pushing too many policies that increase spending and cause burdens on companies. Thus, the poor companies and businesses can't help their employees or unions.

It works for any political party too! In late 2022, the Biden administration signed a bill to block the national U.S. railroad strike because it would have devastated the U.S. economy. The outrageous demands of the railroad workers included actually having sick days, being allowed to see the doctor, and having to work weekslong at a time causing burnout. Thankfully, the workers basically got nothing. Two months later, a train from one of the companies who was blocking the strike (Norfolk Southern), derailed near East Palestine, Ohio spilling hundreds of tons of toxic chemicals that caused a mass evacuation of the town. The executives managed to escape without any punishment, thus no one was harmed in the incident.

The Economy: GDPerfect

Apologies, it seems Bernie Sanders got hold of one of the surveys and participated. The Economy is as strong as ever, ignore the poor, huddled masses over there and look at all these stock charts! They all always go up; it just depends on which way you look at them.

₹ ¥ € ₴ £ $

You Did Start The Fire

Now you have a nice list of people that you can blame instead of everyone pointing the finger at the economy, your company, or – capitalist god forbid – you. There is another tactic you can use that has become even more effective in today's climate.

These days, one of the easiest ways to move the spotlight away from an oligarch is to push the poors into targeting each other. It is time for you to start a culture war.

Starting a culture war is much easier, although it is practically a cake walk if you already own a media conglomerate (as discussed in Chapter 6). In this case, you already have a megaphone to spew massive amounts of hatred and dog whistles. Incidentally, you can also utilize your pocket full of politicians to spew the same garbage and talking points. This type of coordinated effort is often seen with the Republican party as you will see multiple versions of the same tweet from different spokes-people or slightly altered versions of opinion pieces in papers, or speeches on television. It is sort of like when you and your buddies plagiarize the same paper in high school, but you all just change a few words, so it isn't obvious. Of course, it clearly is obvious, but, just like your high school teacher, the general public is too poor and busy to notice, nor care.

So, which culture war? It is the dealer's choice. There are so many of them to choose from today. Plus, you can choose whether to support the woke or anti-woke side of each, depending on where your interests lie. Let's take an example of a few and you can decide which side of the woke aisle is written.

- Education – "Parents clearly know more than the teachers that studied to teach their kids. That is why they should be in charge of what books are allowed in the library – the answer is none. They should also be in charge of what subjects are taught in school – the answer is one: religion."

- Law – "The laws in this country only apply to the have-nots. There is a class in this country that is perpetually kept down by the jackbooted foot soldiers of the government. They should all be put in jail, but not American jail, that is cruel and unusual punishment. Maybe Norwegian jail, it is civil there."

- Gender – "I cannot believe all these companies are coming out to support the LGBTQIA+ agenda. I am greatly offended by these rainbow flags. The rainbow is from God and the gays stole it. They need to give it back to him right now. I'm going to go out and buy all the lite beer I can that has rainbows on it and blow it up, that'll show these companies. Go woke, go broke! Speaking of which, I better get down to the welfare office to grab my paycheck."

Did you guess which one was which in that little quiz? Doesn't matter if you did or didn't. The answer is not a matter of importance. The point is that these types of arguments keep the poor classes rabidly against each other and you can go on exploiting the rest of the world.

Fig. 28: Culture Wars Are More Popular Than Regular
Wars, But Less Popular Than Star Wars

₹ ¥ € ₦ £ $

ESCAPE BY THE SKIN OF YOUR WALLET

Well, you tried all you could, but there is a harsh reality that someday the lower classes could truly revolt. Or so the legend says. If that does occur while you are still alive and haven't been cryogenically frozen for your trip into rich man's space utopia, then you'll need to hide out on Earth. There are a few options for you, which you can learn from other oligarchs who have begun to prepare for the poor people apocalypse.

KANSAS SURVIVAL CONDOS

You read that right. A company outside of Wichita, Kansas has converted an old Atlas ICBM missile silo – located underground – into luxury survival condos for the rich to wait out the apocalypse. These princely underground condos come fully furnished with all the amenities. You would likely want to opt for a penthouse that comes fully customized. There is even a pool and movie theater in the complex. Not bad but it might be a bit on the cheaper side for a rich oligarch like yourself. Plus, there are likely poorer people than you in there and who wants that? Filthy millionaires.

Private Island

Who says that owning a private island is only for leisure? It can also be for escaping the proletariat. Let's face it, they couldn't afford swimming lessons, much less a boat license, right? It is slightly more luxurious than living underground in a refurbished nuclear silo, plus you get a bit of sunshine instead of turning into some billionaire mole person. Your island doesn't have to be some dinky one on an archipelago either. Plus, you can name it yourself. Take for instance, Necker Island. This is owned by Sir Richard Branson, the Virgin mogul (well not so good with getting to space these days). This 74-acre island is in the British Virgin Islands and can be occupied by up to 40 billionaires. Larry Ellison is another great example. In 2012, he bought nearly the entire Hawaiian island of Lanai. Unfortunately, he went altruistic and is turning it into a tourist destination and a better place for the locals to live. But maybe you take the Jeffrey Epstein route of Little Saint James island, if you are into that sort of thing. Most oligarchs have some kink after all, and it usually ain't palatable. Just make sure the cameras are always working on your island in case someone tries to suicide you.

Secret Hidden Town in Germany

Nothing like the German tradition of hiding out in a secret bunker from people trying to kill you. However, in Vivos Europa One, a bunker hidden under a small town in Germany, you'll be living in a bit more luxury than Herr Hitler. And hopefully you won't have to kill yourself. It has been called the world's largest and safest bunker in the world. It was carved out of bedrock under a 400-foot mountain by the Soviets during the Cold War. Sadly, they have since removed the Soviet aesthetic and put in some modernist bull crap. This place has gyms, theatres, restaurants, bars, a hospital, and catastrophic proof doors – which you never get at the Park Hyatt. That place has really let itself go in the past few years.

New Zealand Doomsday Bunkers

You may want to hurry on buying these as they are going like Beanie Babies in the 90s or Toilet Paper in 2020. In 2021, New Zealand was named the most isolated rich country in the world. It has also been at the top of many lists of best places to survive a worldwide apocalypse. Pretty sure Cosmopolitan magazine releases one of those lists annually. Thus, it has become a haven for ultra rich crazy people to buy up large swaths of land and build elaborate doomsday bunkers. Since you aren't an elf, a dwarf, or a hobbit, how do you go about securing one of these luxury doomsday getaways? Well first, you need to buy New Zealand citizenship. As mentioned in an earlier chapter, this is known as the "Golden Passport" or "Golden Visa." New Zealand's price tag was $2 million in 2021. Once you have this, you can use your vast fortune to buy plenty of land and materials. Perhaps in the Southern Alps.

Some big-name oligarchs have taken advantage of New Zealand and built doomsday palaces. These include Steve Hoffman, co-CEO of Reddit (so you can imagine how deranged his bunker must be), Larry Page, co-founder of Google, and Peter Thiel, founder of PayPal. Peter Thiel bought his share in New Zealand after the 2008 presidential election victory of Barack Obama. He clearly saw that as the beginning of the end. He seems to hate black people so much that a black president made him literally flee across the Pacific Ocean. This same motivation for the poor may apply to you. If that is the case, New Zealand is a great place to build your secret bunker. There are plenty of companies that tout bulletproof windows, concrete-reinforced walls, state-of-the-art surveillance systems, and of course what every bunker needs, a rumpus room. The added bonus for moving there is that you can get another chance of learning how the fuck to play rugby if you didn't when you hid your money in Samoa.

Unfortunately, there still hasn't been a way to simply launch all the poor into space. You will have to continue to "share" this planet with them for now. However, with the tactics above, hopefully you can keep them docile enough to avoid any scary complaints, protests, strikes, or god forbid – socialist revolts. With these tools in your rhinestone belt, let's move on to the final chapter of your oligarch career, collecting all the remaining spoils left on Earth to reach the tippy top of the golden pyramid.

Chapter 10

Spoils For The Spoiled

"The only thing that could spoil a day was people."

— Ernest Hemingway, Drunkard

You did it! You have reached the very top of the oligarchy. Breathe in the rarefied air, then be sure to bottle it and sell it to the masses choking on the factory fumes that your companies are spewing out without concern. So, what do you do now? Well friend, there are still things to take from others. Why should they have anything after all? Now though, these things are much bigger and much more necessary for people to live. You have become the master of the universe. It is time to gut that universe and sell it for parts.

This Land Is My Land

You may be asking, why do I need land? I have ten houses across the world, thousands of acres where I can build my doomsday bunkers or hunt humans for sport, and several golf courses to get in a quick 18 holes after hunting. But is that really enough? No, it will never be enough. There is an empty hole inside of you that cannot be filled. You can try to fill it though, and stealing land from others is a great activity to fill your spare time.

This is known as "land grabbing" where companies, governments, and oligarchs like yourself buy out massive pieces of land. More often than not, the land that you buy has people living on it, working on it, and enjoying its ample provisions. Those should be your ample provisions. Well, with your deep pockets, political influence, and lack of even a shred of empathy, it will be yours. The tradition of land grabbing goes back at least a century, especially in Latin America and Southeast Asia. Let's see how to do this by looking at a few others who stole pastures in the past.

Dole: Pineapple Express

Originally known as the Hawaiian Pineapple Company, Dole was founded in 1901 by James Dole and within 50 years, he had become known as the "King of Pineapple" for the company's massive success at canning and selling pineapple around the world. James Dole's legacy lives on today in white people making depressing morning smoothies across suburbia.

However, the story starts a bit earlier than that. His father, Sanford Dole, led a group of sugarcane and pineapple growers, enlisted the U.S. Army, and overthrew Queen Liliuokalani in a coup. He then decided he would be King of Hawaii and the U.S. government, led by President Grover Cleveland, left him alone. By 1898, Dole had convinced the government to completely annex the islands. The Dole family would reap the awards of this pineapple paradise and America got a new territory that would eventually become the 50th state. That state eventually led to the inspiration for the 2016 Disney film, Moana. So, you can thank capitalist barons like the Doles for giving us that Disney classic. In fact, the song "How Far I'll Go" is actually about how far the Doles would go to reap those sweet pineapple profits. The more you know.

Now, you may not be able to wrangle an entire state anymore out of your landgrab – although one of the U.S. southern states may sell you theirs at this rate. You can also grab land abroad with a little help from the American government of course.

CHIQUITA: TALLY ME BANANA

Yep, another fruit company. The agricultural oligarchs really dominate this field – and the fields of sovereign nations. No reason you can't get into the avocado game someday. This example is actually the first of where we get "Banana Republic." The clothing store, not the event where a sovereign nation is ostensibly taken over by a large corporation and run like a private enterprise. It could be both, but that just seems like a coincidence. Chiquita was originally known as the United Fruit Company (curious why these companies keep changing their names). United Fruit was a banana conglomerate that emerged at the turn of the 20th century, muscling out other banana producers around the world to gain a global monopoly. Without any private competition, they decided to start competing with the public. Part of this strategy was to pay off local officials and military leaders to gain exclusive land rights. This proved fruitful (heh), until some liberals in Guatemala decided that they wanted to use their own country's land for themselves. After they took over, United Fruit was due to lose 1.5 million acres of its rightfully bribed land. That was unacceptable, the land couldn't go back to those tens of thousands of displaced Guatemalan families.

Fig. 29: Bananas With The CIA's Original Logo From 1953 - 1961

What did United Fruit do? Well it called on its old friend, the USA, who rather than send troops like with Dole decades earlier, called in its new agency, the CIA. Known as Operation PBSUC-CESS, the CIA and United Fruit supported an opposition who managed to force the government to resign in 1954. He was replaced by a CIA-picked dictator and surprisingly an enthusiast of providing a whole bunch of banana-growing land to United Fruit. Today, Chiquita still owns that land, so this story has a happy ending.

WATERWORLD

In the documentary film, *Quantum of Solace*, the narrator, Daniel Craig, is attempting to learn about a man who is trying to steal the water supply of a country. Sadly, that man fails to steal the water because Bond gets in the way, selfish Brit that he is.

There may not be anything as appropriately oligarchic as taking people's water away and charging them for it. Water is the most necessary of resources on Earth that all humans – except for the dried husk that is Rupert Murdoch – require to survive. From drinking water to agriculture to sewage to watering lawns for some pointless reason, water is used by everyone, everywhere. There is no better resource to monopolize than H20. Let's learn how others have – and are continuing to – siphon off water supplies from the rest of the world.

WONDERFUL PISTACHIO COMPANY: TURNING BLUE TO GREEN

Owned by Lynda and Stewart Resnick since the late 1970s, the Wonderful company has done a great job at stealing as much water as possible from the public. They also own FIJI Water, a bottled water that takes 1.75 gallons per bottle to package and ship from the island in the South Pacific. An island where more than 10 percent do not have access to clean drinking water. But that is a different story. For now, let's focus on their vast pistachio and almond empire in the Western United States.

The Resnicks' company, worth $4.2 billion, is the second largest produce company in the world. And if there is one thing that crops need, its water. Pistachios and almonds need excessive amounts of water, like they are perpetually trying to get over a hangover. The Resnicks have cleverly maneuvered their way into backroom politics and obscure water rights law. In 2015, they donated nearly $50 million to political campaigns. It is now believed that they consume more water than every household and company in California. Some estimates say they use more water than all the residents of Los Angeles and San Francisco – combined. Sometimes they just leave the faucet on for fun.

Even during some of the worst droughts that California has seen in the past decade, the Resnicks have still managed to expand their farms and the water that they consume. In 2020, the Resnicks (and one of their suppliers) ended up in a tiff with the U.S. Navy as their pistachio farms were taking more of the ground water supply that the nearby Naval base needed, causing much anger and gnashing of teeth. So, local officials stepped in...to help the Resnicks. They clearly know where the real power lies. It's in the nut. Pistachios and almonds do pack a lot of energy in them. Those are just facts. Wonderful facts.

NESTLE: OLIGARCHY IN A BOTTLE

Often voted as one of the evilest companies in the world by the lower classes, Nestle has garnered an elite reputation as a premier oligarchic enterprise. It is difficult to decide where to even start discussing Nestle's various exploitations around the globe. This is one company where you will definitely want to write down some strategies to support your empire.

Much like their Native American cousins in America, the First Nations of Canada never had to deal with any strife. However, that finally came to an end in the last couple of decades. In 2016, Nestle outbid a small municipality near Ontario to buy the town's well. It has since extracted millions of liters of water and sold it bottled. The locals have lacked running water since then. However, they do have all the clean, bottled water they can get. For a price, of course.

Flying over to the Middle East and Africa, Nestle has continued to bring its gospel of the bottled water to the people in places like Pakistan and Nigeria. For instance, Nestle drained the entire water supply for a village in Pakistan for their bottled water. Thousands got sick. They then took that bottled water and sold it the city of Lahore. Often, Nestle is able to buy the rights to water sources for mere pennies, sometimes as low as $4 for 1 million liters. They have continued to hoard water around the world, targeting third world countries in Africa, Latin America, Asia, and Flint, Michigan.

Water is a fundamental human right, but it is time you make it a privilege for the people. Take the lessons from Wonderful and Nestle to start making regular folks work for one of the few things that is necessary to keep them alive. It is also easy to make a brand of bottled water that sounds refreshing without letting people know that it is being taken from the thirsty poor. A few examples you could use are Rushing Meadows Spring Water, Acqua Aristocrata, or the French brand of Poorier.

Between A Rock and A Rich Place

Metals, Gas, Oil, Gems. The four horsemen of the oligarchic apocalypse. In the last two decades, companies in these industries have consumed the third world like they were Augustus Gloop sucking down chocolate in Willy Wonka's factory. This has become easier as the companies provide exorbitant amounts of money to governments for the rights to drill or mine in their countries. Most of that money goes into the pockets of the government and little into investing in the people, except for great jobs with little pay in harsh drilling environments! Whether you need some gold for the circuitry in your Tesla, or gas if you need to fill up your Ford 150XXL, or if you need to buy a diamond for your third wedding, chances are these companies are helping you do it. Let's see what secrets you can learn from the experts to exploit this market.

Shell: Dutch Courage

The Shell Corporation has done an admirable job in the past thirty or forty years of exploiting Africa. The Shell Corporation started exploring for oil in Nigeria in the late 1930s. By 1958, they had discovered several fields and cashed in their exploration "licenses" to start drilling and exporting the black gold. They have continued to profit from plenty of different sites across the continent. In the first three months of 2023, Shell made almost $10 billion in profit (after expenses). That is the most they have ever made as profit and only in the first 25 percent of the year. They took that money and invested it in the community. Of course, the community is the Shell shareholders.

Shell has worked to help other communities in Africa as well, mostly by building pipelines through their properties and then asking the government to give them full rights to said properties. It's not like the citizens who live on those lands are growing anything. This is mostly due to extreme climate change events that have caused extended droughts or massive floods. These events have resulted in little to no crop yield for the farmers. That's OK though, they have plenty of crude oil to drink and feed their families with during these hard times.

Shell has one of its largest oil operations in the Niger Delta, and it has only had a few hundred oil spills per year. That is above the lowest bar ever for oil companies. The residents of towns near the drilling areas tend to face such lovely benefits as high poverty rates, a degraded environment, and an excess of disease. Any exploited town would kill – well, would be killed – to have these same benefits. Shell offers them for free, just at the expensive of the government's integrity and the environments integrity... and the people's integrity. It could be worse, not sure how, but it could be. Shell has been criticized by Amnesty International for violating human rights, including encouraging the military to protect their assets by engaging in extrajudicial killings among other transgressions – like overcooking pasta. Shell responded to the report by drilling even more into the country. Shell just doesn't know when "No" means "No." They have the profit to prove it.

Anglo American: Digging Deep

The mining consortium and properly named, Anglo American, has been a major player in targeting African countries for mining (Rio Tinto is the equivalent company in South America). The company is actually a British multinational, so it is easy for them to re-colonialize the countries where their sweet minerals and liquids are available. They have "bought" land in Botswana, Mozambique, and Namibia to support their mining of cement, iron ore, coal, zinc, magic beans, lead, bitcoins, and aluminum. They have destroyed nearly a million acres of soil – who needs farming anyway. People can just live off any leftover water droplets on the ore rocks. Pretty sure that is how geology works. This destruction now threatens to make millions of people in Southern Africa homeless (or landless) and starving.

If you managed to grab some water sources at this point, you are far ahead of any of the actual denizens of Africa. Everyone is ahead of them at this point.

It's A House Party: Blackstone

Blackstone (not to be confused with Blackrock, a similar company) is known as an asset investment company. Basically, they produce nothing of value to anyone outside of their share-holders. There only goal is to buy up companies and other assets (e.g., commercial buildings, apartment buildings, capital for mortgages) that they can then either rent out to others or sell for a profit. Blackstone has often been considered one of the most powerful companies in the world given its massive assets and its unique ability to operate mostly under the public's radar. You may have heard of the company, but do you really know what it does other than what you just read? Exactly. As of 2022, they managed nearly $10 billion in assets and had over 200 companies under there umbrella that they have bought up.

In the past few years, especially as the housing crises came to a head before, during, and immediately after the pandemic, Blackstone has been diligently buying up family homes in the thousands around the United States. Additionally, they are also buying up home credit lines and real estate companies to continue expanding their grip on the real estate market.

Pretium Partners

This massive NY-based real estate company has been buying up homes like hotcakes over the last few years. During the pandemic, Zillow, another company, attempted to break into the market. Zillow would pay all cash upfront on homes around the country. Its intent was to turn them into rentals, because the younger generations will never be able to afford their own home. They will rent until they die. Zillow mistimed the market and ended up buying more than it could rent. Pretium took these homes off their hands for dirt cheap prices and gave them to the homeless. But not really. The younger generations will still have to rent forever, just to a different oligarch instead.

In 2023, Pretium again bought thousands of homes to the tune of $1.5 billion with the same intent of renting them to the middle and lower classes. In this way, they can continue to raise the rents each year and thus the poor never build equity, develop credit, or own anything. Think of it like streaming services or when you buy a movie off Amazon Prime, you never really own those either.

In the glorious oligarch future, the lesser classes will rent everything. From entertainment, to housing, to food, water, and any other basic necessities that can be monetized (hint, its all of them if you truly believe). Only you will own everything and that is what being a true oligarch is all about. It's about the friends we rented along the way.

₹ ¥ € ₪ £ $

From Crisis To Opportunity

When Alexander the Great looked out across his domain, he was quoted as sighing and saying, "There are no more worlds to conquer." He just wasn't thinking big enough. That is probably why he is dead. There is one final area that you can conquer – worldwide disasters and events. That's right, you can make plenty of profit off of mother nature's back as well as the backs of bloody conflict. This is sometimes referred to as "shock therapy," where companies take advantage of a "shock" to society or the environment to make extra profit. Let's take a look at this final bastion of profit, whose doors are ready to be broken down for good.

Drought: Parched Lips Build Ships

It's time to revisit your favorite evil corporation again, Nestle. In California, droughts have become more commonplace in the past decade due to some scientist-made-up thing called climate change. Nestle has taken advantage of these droughts, particularly in 2021. As the state's scarce water resources dried up and forced citizens to limit their water use, Nestle continued to siphon millions of gallons of it out of the San Bernadino Forest. The river they were taking it from provides drinking water to around 800,000 residents. When the government complained, Nestle claimed that they had the right to take the water for bottling since 1865. Who can forget how California miners would sip on a refreshing Nestle water bottle after panning for gold all day. The government is trying to fine the company up to $10,000 a day for its illegal siphoning. That will show that multi-billion-dollar company. They could make that in a day selling bottled water to the citizens whose drinking water they are taking. That's just good business.

Pandemic: Cash Is Contagious

COVID-19 killed millions around the world and reminded everyone about the dangers of vaccines and 5G. It also gave corporations a chance to act like a virus too. Many corporations managed to gain record profits and at the same time had the government forgive loans from the Paycheck Protection Program (PPP) that was designed to help smaller businesses weather the pandemic during government-mandated shutdowns. Take for instance the Houston company, Sharps Compliance. As a medical waste company, they were needed to help clean up used needles from vaccines. Their executives received double their salary in 2021 and at the same time, they managed to get $2 million in PPP loans forgiven.

Financial Technology (FinTech) firms – who tend to have the absolute stupidest names – also benefitted greatly in this environment. Many of them were tasked by the government to administer the PPP loans. Instead, they often would pocket a hefty amount of the loans that were destined for smaller businesses. One company, Kabbage (see how stupid these names are?), approved hundreds of PPP loans for fake farms, including an orange grove in Minnesota. They didn't even bother making them look legitimate as there was no fraud control from the government. Who doesn't love a delicious Duluth, Minnesota orange though?

Hurricane: A Category 5 Opportunity

This is a great disaster for you to take advantage of because they are so frequent and becoming more powerful due to climate change. You can be sure that on an annual basis, you will get at least one that makes damaging landfall in the Caribbean or the United States. Of course, one of the most famous, Hurricane Katrina, which laid waste to New Orleans in 2005, also broke open the levees of companies seeking to make a quick buck.

Private military contractors – particularly Erik Prince's Black-water – made a significant profit by providing security services to the rich of New Orleans. One report noted that Blackwater killed 38 looters in different neighborhoods. Come on, these poor people just lost everything, you can't let them have your precious things. The rest of the citizens were fine in the New Orleans Super Dome with water provided by Nestle.

Other companies tend to flock to hurricanes with investment scams. This involves getting your average Jane or Joe to donate money to the company to help with cleanup services. Of course, these services never happen. The only cleaning they are doing is cleaning out sucker's wallets.

War: All Profit On The Western Front

Companies have been profiteering on wars for centuries. Many even goad countries into war precisely to make a profit. There is never a shortage of people who want to kill each other and thus there will never be a shortage of opportunities for you to add to your coffers faster than these people are added to coffins.

The U.S. military industrial complex is basically a corporate slush fund for companies that make weapons or – even more profitable – provide all the other services needed for an army. These include food, clothing, shelter, and latrines. The Department of Defense (DoD) budget in 2023 was $2.1 trillion (yes, with a T). It is these outrageous budgets that led to things like $90 individual screws. That $2.1 trillion is also a peacetime budget, so you can imagine how much more it balloons to when the U.S. is engaged in an active war.

The 2003 War in Iraq where they totally found all those Weapons of Mass Destruction (WMDs) is a textbook example of how much profit you truly can make during conflict. The top ten contractors providing services to the army made at least $72 billion between them. Probably the most famous is Halliburton. The U.S. Vice President at the time, Dick Cheney, had been a top executive at Halliburton before. Even conflicts of interest pay well. They received a hefty contract to build the gated resort community at Guantanamo Bay. Also at that time, the government gave $50,000 to a private company to investigate the bomb-detecting capabilities of African elephants, which went about as well as you can imagine. Probably the most brilliant piece of profit was a $640 toilet seat that the government was happy to shell out for soldiers in the war. That's the geese that laid the golden turd for sure.

Fig. 30: Dick Cheney, Seen Here Trying To Push One Out On His $640 Toilet Seat

The most recent war between Ukraine and Russia saw a nearly 50 percent increase in profits for natural resource providers – mostly coal and oil. As Russia cut off its oil pipeline to Europe, prices went up along with profits. Rather than cut prices to help people get through the winter, companies said fuck you pay me more. Its basic business and the people cannot do anything about it. Thanks Putin!

The beauty of exploiting crises like natural disasters and wars is it basically provides you with limitless opportunities to make more money for your oligarchic needs. Resources can be diminished, so you may not always be able to drill on natural preserves or steal the water from needy communities. But as climate change worsens, natural disasters become more damaging, and conflicts become more common. And thus, so do your profits.

₹ ¥ € ₴ £ $

A Life Of Leisure

Now that you have reached the top, what else is there to do? Why not take some time for yourself? It's time to find some new hobbies. But you are an oligarch, you aren't going to pick up crochet or build model trains. No, you need something more exciting to fit your lifestyle. Let's look at some of the best pastimes to engage yourself in to fill that bottomless void inside of you.

Patron of the Arts

Isn't about time you invested in pretty colors that are framed on your wall? Time to take down that Counting Crows poster, frame it, and put it back up. But you should take down that *Breakfast at Tiffany's* poster and replace it. It's not like you ever saw that movie.

Art is a great way to show that you care about culture, even if you don't. Even better, art is a well-known way to launder or hide your money. There are plenty of billionaire oligarchs that buy art for millions only to keep it stored in a secure facility.

The founder of the hedge fund Citadel, Ken Griffin, likes to pay lots of money for lots of art. His biggest purchases have been in the hundreds of millions of dollars. Sometimes these oligarchs just swap paintings from each other in private sales. It is like spouse swapping, but with less bodily fluids.

Car Collecting

What better way to show off your wealth while contributing more pollution to the environment? You can go the route of collecting exotic cars like Bill Gates, Elon Musk, and Jeff Bezos do. Some of these include the $2 million Bugatti Veyron, which isn't even street legal in many places. Although, that shouldn't stop you from driving around public-school zones.

Or perhaps you want to go for quantity over quality and own an obscene amount of cars that you couldn't possibly ever drive in a lifetime. The Sultan of Brunei owns around 7,000 cars worth an estimated $5 billion. There is also Sheikh Hamad Bin Hamdan Al Nahyan, part of the ruling elite in Abu Dhabi, who has thousands of cars, including a collection of monster trucks. It is rumored he uses these monster trucks to run over any dissidents speaking against the royal family. That is a pretty entertaining way to keep the lower classes in check while simultaneously entertaining them too. The poor do love monster truck rallies after all.

Big Game Hunting

Ok, so maybe you want to collect something a bit more interesting, like the heads and pelts of exotic animals. It might be frowned upon by the general populace, but why would you care what they think? They tend to frown on everything you do anyway.

Countries like Zimbabwe and South Africa offer legal licenses for hunting big game, so you have the opportunity to grab yourself a few lion furs and maybe an elephant horn or two. They are good for virility according to the not-at-all quack doctors of Chinese medicine. However, is it really all that fun if it is legal? No, you want to hunt endangered animals like the black rhino, the mountain gorilla, the tiger, or the moral politician. So grab your laser-guided high-powered rifle, hop in your helicopter, and mow down some giant pandas. It will be the best safari you ever take.

Running For President

This may not seem like the best use of your time, especially because you can usually buy all the politicians you need. However, you may want to hop into the game for a bit of grifting. Plenty of far stupider oligarchs have tried their luck at the presidency. Hell, one even became a president (although his billionaire status is highly questionable). Either way, he made a whole bunch more money through campaign donations from the most gullible poor people. Another billionaire that tried his luck was Michael Bloomberg. Bloomberg is about as human and likeable as black mold. During the 2016 primaries, he spent an estimated $1 billion on his campaign only to ever gain a few measly percentage points in the polls. Don't be like Bloomberg.

You could also run as a third-party candidate like Ross Perot did in the 1992 election. He was able to siphon off the most votes any third-party candidate ever has in a political race. Perhaps if you put enough money in, you could actually win without having to deal with the other parties. Again though, it is still easier to simply buy the other parties, just not as exciting.

Pedophilia and Human Trafficking

Those other hobbies may still not be exciting enough for you. Well, there is a final one that is one of the biggest hits with all the oligarchs around the world. Having sex with children. So wholesome. Perhaps you may even find the children that you sold way back in Chapter 3. It'll be quite the family reunion.

Although Jeffrey Epstein is now gone and his islands are up for sale, his clientele has remained a mystery. Although the flight logs of big names like Bill Gates, Bill Clinton, Prince Andrew of the British Royal Family, and Elon Musk have shown up flying to his island. But maybe they were just going for a fun snorkeling trip. Either way, there remains a non-zero chance that similar child trafficking rings exist around the world. And Liam Neeson is getting a little bit up there in age, so you wouldn't have to worry too much about him taking them or you out. Especially if you refrain from taking any more of his children.

Rocket Off To Space

Of course, it would be remiss if you didn't consider starting your own space company to build rockets to space, the moon, and Mars. Richard Branson (Virgin Galactic), Jeff Bezos (Blue Origin), and Elon Musk (Space X) have all decided to use their vast wealth for the greatest dick-measuring contest of all time. Why waste it on helping the rest of the world when you can just escape it when the time comes. Even better, you can win big, juicy government contracts to subsidize your company, so you don't even have to put your own money into the venture! Bang, zoom, straight to the Moon and straight to your wallet.

There really is no limit to what you want to do with your leisure time, only your imagination. With the amount of money and power you have, the world – nay the universe – is your playground. For as long as it still exists of course. So, go out, exploit, eliminate, and enjoy, my dear oligarch.

CASHING IN AND CASHING OUT

You have conquered the world and are the one true oligarch. You have won capitalism. As you know, once you win capitalism, you immediately ascend to Ayn Rynd Heaven. Have you not yet? Well, it is coming. Don't you worry. Everyone knows that whoever has the most things at the end is declared the winner.

Unfortunately, the one thing that oligarchs have not conquered is time and the inevitable decaying procession toward death. Despite the best efforts of wealthy men in the past, they have still had to face the grave – or in most cases the opulent mausoleum built by contractors that were never paid for their labor.

However, there is hope. Billionaires like Larry Ellison and Peter Thiel are investing loads of money into anti-aging research and biotechnology in an attempt to pause the aging process and live forever. Others like them are sometimes known as "immortalists." They want to not only live forever, but rule forever in their late-stage capitalist paradise. Does that mean they want to try and preserve the planet they would live on forever? Of course not, they will just live in space or find the next planet to colonize with their human and robot slaves. Elon Musk has said as much for his plan to colonize Mars. Although, at this point he can't even run a social media company. At this point, he may not be able to run a bath.

You, too, can use your funds for this research in an attempt to preserve your ever-aging body. Or to invest in cryogenics and freeze your gross body until a cure for aging is found. You would have to rely on others for this though, so that may not be the best option.

If you must face the grim reaper (who only ever wears a robe, sounds sort of poor), you have to consider what to do with your wealth when you pass on. If you have any heirs, you could leave it to them. Although, it is likely that they, or their grandchildren will blow it all because they are spoiled idiots. Not your fault, you didn't raise them.

You could give it to charity like Bill Gates and Warren Buffet plan to do. But then what was all this for? You did all this work to become an oligarch only to give it back to the poor? That's no legacy for an oligarch.

No, the best thing to do is try and live forever. Barring that, take it all with you and shoot yourself into space. Perhaps an alien species will discover you and you can introduce them to the fabulous benefits of capitalism – and then exploit them with it.

Whatever you decide, know that you have become the master of this planet. You, dear oligarch, have done what few in the history of mankind have done. Made the most money ever.

To conclude with a quote from F. Scott Fitzgerald about another true capitalist, Jay Gatsby:

"Gatsby believed in the green light, the orgasmic future that year by year recedes before us. It eluded us then, but that's no matter—tomorrow we will profit faster, exploit further, destroy unions more fully, and beat the poor even harder.

So we beat on, super yachts against the current, borne back ceaselessly into the past."

So beat on, dear lover of capitalism, for you are the Greatest Gatsby. You are the greatest oligarch.

Want to keep reading?

Subscribe now, find out how this book ends while gaining *Unlimited Digital Access* to the Entire Outro for only $19.99/month/*12/*lifetime

SUBSCRIBE NOW

The author had planned to use detailed citations, but the designer wanted even *more* money. Instead, the end-notes have been sold out to advertisers, so screw that guy and grab a bag of Flamin' Hot Cheetos before diving in, they are Dangerously Cheesy!

1. Are you looking for pockets on your leggings? Trousers that cling? Shorts that go to your socks? Lululemon has you covered with the all-new Align High Rise Omni-pant, now just $128! Online *only!*

2. You don't want tuna with good taste, but tuna that tastes good. Starkist Brand Tuna: *Overfish'd 'til it's delisch'.*

3. There are some things money can't buy... like people. For everything else, including people, there's Mastercard.

4. Got somewhere to be? We'll get you there only two hours late. Amtrak: Stay a while.

5. Feeling depressed? Cymbalta® can help. Ask your doctor now about Cymbalta®. Ask him. Now. I mean, literally now. Ask him now, he's on the ceiling - look. ASK HIM. Disclaimer: Cymbalta® may cause diarrhoea, depression and moderate to severe hallucinations.

6. Order Pizza Hut For Your Next Socialist Party. No One Out Pizzas The Hut. Not Even The Opposition.

7. Do you wish *your* breath could smell as nice as being rich feels? Well, make sure you don't have poor people breath, grab a stick of doublemint today!

8. You Might Not Be Able To Afford A Doomsday Bunker, But You Can Stay At A Holiday Inn Express *Tonight*. Yaaaaaaay.

9. Covalaxaproxinehydroclorapralax™: Get Your Sixteenth New and Improved Booster Shot Today, now with extra lead for 5G protection.

Appendix: The Great Exploiters of Earth

There are plenty of distinguished oligarchs who have adorned the golden-plated halls of capitalism. The following pages list some of the most well-known – as well as some of the lesser-known examples of these great hoarders of wealth. Never be afraid to steal characteristics, ideas, and hobbies from them; they would appreciate it and do the same to you if they could. Although beware, some may try to charge you or sue you, so always have your team of lawyers ready. This list is non-exhaustive, but it contains many of the OG Russian oligarchs, the crazed capitalists, the magnificent monopolists, and the beautiful bourgeoisie. These are the pioneers who paved the way, leaving in their wake dead union leaders, broken promises, gutted companies, impoverished nations, and polluted environments, but most importantly, opportunities for future oligarchs like yourself to flourish.

*Not just a
blank page!*

This almost
entirely
white space
is proudly
sponsored by
the Ayn Rand
Literary
Appreciation
Society

*"Atlas Shrugged
should have
been longer!"*

Mukesh Ambani

Net Worth: $91 Billion
Company: Reliance Industries
Industry: Energy, Chemicals, Telecom, Gas
Country: India
Cause of Wealth: Helping Daddy With His Business
Interests: Stock Manipulation, Jets, Mocktails
Favorite Purchase: $1 Billion Personal Apartment Tower known as "Antilla"
Summary: One of the richest men in Asia, Ambani built a massive conglomerate over the last several decades. The Indian government even gave him Z-level clearance, which gives him elite government commandos as his security team. Ambani is infamous for building a $1billion tower for his family that looks over the slums of Mumbai. Comes complete with 660 servants. Never can have enough.

BERNARD ARNAULT

Net Worth: $225 Billion
Company: LVMH Moet Hennessy Louis Vuitton
Industry: Alcohol, Fancy Handbags
Country: France
Cause of Wealth: Hip-Hop Videos
Interests: Avoiding Taxes, Collecting Expensive Art, Playing Chess Like A Dweeb
Favorite Purchase: 135-Acre Private Island
Summary: One of the "quiet billionaires," Arnault only has become more well-known after briefly claiming the spot for richest person in the world over Elon Musk in early 2023. He has been nicknamed "The Terminator" for laying off over 9000 workers when first acquiring a company. Quiet, but ruthless. He also built a foundation with the help from the always benevolent Vladimir Putin.

Francoise Bettencourt Meyers

Net Worth: $90 Billion
Company: L'Oréal
Industry: Cosmetics
Country: France
Cause of Wealth: Forced Her Inheritance
Interests: Catholicism for a bit, then Judaism, then just money
Favorite Purchase: An Australian Soap Company
Summary: A noted recluse, Francoise inherited her fortune after secretly recording her mother to declare her incompetent in court. She was once a devout Catholic that wrote about bible verses. Her grandfather was a well-known collaborator with the Nazis, making her switch to Judaism rather controversial. But who cares, she is rich.

Jeffrey Bezos

Net Worth: $150 Billion
Company: Amazon, Blue Origin
Industry: E-Commerce, Space Travel
Country: United States
Cause of Wealth: Parental Loan and Modern Slavery
Interests: Being A Space Cowboy, Sleeping, Avoiding Paying Livable Wages
Favorite Purchase: The Washington Post
Summary: With a smile as shiny as his head, Bezos has enjoyed over twenty years at the top of the oligarch food chain, even going as far as buying Whole Foods. When he isn't paying governments to remove bridges so he can move his superyacht out of their harbor, he loves spending time finding new ways to squeeze more profits out of his workers.

Michael Bloomberg

Net Worth: $95 Billion
Company: Bloomberg LP
Industry: Financial Information & Media
Country: United States
Cause of Wealth: Shady Investing
Interests: Being Mayor, Being President, Being Likeable. He is 1 for 3
Favorite Purchase: Political Advertising
Summary: A lifelong New Yorker who made his immense wealth trading on Wall Street before deciding to just build a trading platform. Bloomberg has achieved other notable things such as banning smoking, banning trans fats, and helping African Americans be far more scared of the police. Stop, frisk, and enjoy a Bloomberg life.

Warren Buffet

Net Worth: $118 Billion
Company: Berkshire Hathaway
Industry: Insurance
Country: United States
Cause of Wealth: Investing at 11 years old
Interests: Ukulele, Werther's Originals, Death Metal
Favorite Purchase: His home for $33,000
Summary: Known as the "Oracle of Omaha," Buffet started paying taxes at 13 like a dope. He continues to teach children how to get rich, so he must be stopped. Although called America's Favorite Tycoon, he has participated in several anticompetitive practices in banking and tech industries. So, there is still an oligarch beyond those thick-framed glasses.

OLEG DERIPESKA

Net Worth: $2.6 Billion (That is known)
Company: RUSAL
Industry: Aluminum
Country: Russia
Cause of Wealth: Privatized State-Owned Assets
Interests: Organized Crime, Play Dates With Putin, Avoiding Sanctions
Favorite Purchase: Cypriot Citizenship
Summary: An OG Russian oligarch, Deripeska has had close ties with Vladimir Putin since he became Russian president for life. He has been linked to influencing U.S. elections via Paul Manafort to further Russian interests. He has a collection of sanctions that sits on his mantel next to his badminton trophies.

LARRY ELLISON

Net Worth: $146 Billion
Company: Oracle
Industry: Software
Country: United States
Cause of Wealth: Boring Business Shit
Interests: The Van Dyke, Japanese Stuff, Funding Failed Republican Candidates
Favorite Purchase: Hawaiian Island of Lanai
Summary: Founder of Oracle, which is either a company that makes databases or a database that makes companies. Ellison is the near the top of the billionaire list. A college dropout, he is famous for spending billions on expensive toys like yachts, planes, and politicians. He is known to have been a part of conversations around overturning 2020 election results.

Bill Gates

Net Worth: $117 Billion
Company: Microsoft
Industry: Computers & Technology
Country: United States
Cause of Wealth: Monopolistic Practices
Interests: Settlers of Catan, Reading, Hanging with Jeffrey Epstein
Favorite Purchase: Horse Farm
Summary: Mr. Microsoft has had his name synonymous with wealth for the better part of four decades after conquering the PC market in the 1980s. He has since tried to whitewash his wealthy history by being noble and trying to cure diseases in third world countries. Although he has been known to be creepy with his employees in the past. Who would have thunk it?

Jack Ma

Net Worth: $24 Billion
Company: Alibaba Group
Industry: E-commerce
Country: China
Cause of Wealth: A Little Help From The CCP
Interests: Painting, Paying Fines to the CCP, Lying Low
Favorite Purchase: Rockefeller's Adirondacks Estate
Summary: A former English teacher, Jack Ma founded Alibaba with some pals in 1999. He is like the Jeff Bezos of China, but probably more likeable, which is a low bar. In 2022, he ran into trouble with the Chinese government – who helped him start the company – for being too rich and fled to Hong Kong to teach. He returned in 2023 to test his luck again.

Elon Musk

Net Worth: $230 Billion
Company: Tesla, Twitter, SpaceX, Boring Company
Industry: Being A Twat
Country: United States (Origin: South Africa)
Cause of Wealth: Daddy's Emerald Mine
Interests: Trolling, Bad Investments, Potential Pedophilia, Anti-Semitism
Favorite Purchase: Twitter (X)
Summary: The on-again, off-again richest person in the world has been spending his wealth on the most important things in life. Mainly, ensuring everyone says nice things about him on social media. Musk, who has 14 children, most of which don't talk to him, has continued to sully his reputation as a tech genius. He continues to make money while embracing the QAnon group. Marshmallow man likes conspiracies.

Johann Rupert

Net Worth: $12 Billion
Company: Compagnie Financière Richemont
Industry: Swiss Luxury Goods
Country: South Africa
Cause of Wealth: Apartheid Inheritance
Interests: Golf, Wine, Racism
Favorite Purchase: Cartier
Summary: Doing the white man proud, Johann recently became the richest African in the world. He inherited his vast empire from his father, who had started a tobacco company in the 1940s. Johann, an Afrikaner, has been linked to excessive racism. Wow, what a surprise. This fat oaf has continued to increase his wealth through luxury sales. He was elected into the South African sports hall of fame, so clearly the country is having some struggles.

CARLOS SLIM

Net Worth: 100+ Billion
Company: America Movil
Industry: Telecommunications
Country: Mexico
Cause of Wealth: Monopoly on State Asset
Interests: Stifling Competition, Baseball, Morgan's Moustache Cream
Favorite Purchase: 417 5th Avenue
Summary: Known as "Mr. Monopoly" in Mexico, Carlos made his fortune by taking a controlling interest in Mexico's telecommunications industry. His net worth is equivalent to 7 percent of Mexico's GDP, which in the United States would be the equivalent of being a trillionaire. He even bailed out the New York Times. Yet, he still drives himself to work, whatever the hell work that is at this point.

ROB WALTON

Net Worth: $64 Billion
Company: Walmart
Industry: Retail
Country: United States
Cause of Wealth: Discount Prices from Inheritance
Interests: Vintage Cars, Dismantling Unions, Soup
Favorite Purchase: Denver Broncos
Summary: The heir of Sam Walton, founder of Walmart, Robson (yes his real name) has remained one of the richest people – and of all the Walton heirs – in the world. Although he is now the former chairman of the retail conglomerate, he continues to work hard to ensure that Walmart's employees do not unionize or have any semblance of rights. He embodies the oligarch spirit.

Bruce Wayne

Net Worth: $10 Billion+
Company: Wayne Enterprises
Industry: Technology, Biotech, Shipping
Country: United States
Cause of Wealth: Murdered Parents
Interests: Spandex, Bats, Emo Music
Favorite Purchase: Bat Nipple Clamps
Summary: Because he hated the opera, Bruce got his parents killed in an alley. It was all a clever ploy to take over their vast empire. He continues to use this empire to give money to charity while at the same time destroying half of Gotham fighting people who don't like him because he is wealthy. Bruce is fighting for oligarchs everywhere by night.

Mark Zuckerberg

Net Worth: $100 Billion
Company: Meta (Facebook, Instagram)
Industry: Social Media, Destruction of Society
Country: Unknown
Cause of Wealth: Stolen Technology
Interests: People's Data, Augustus Caesar, Delicious Flies
Favorite Purchase: Instagram
Summary: The lizard king of social media dropped out of Harvard after stealing the overall platform that would become Facebook. More recently, Zuckerberg has enjoyed selling user's private data to governments and companies for a profit. In addition, he continues to push his Meta platform to have people work in Virtual Reality akin to a cheaper Sims game.

Recommended Reading

Ayn, Rand, "Atlas Shrugged"
Smith, Adam, "The Wealth of Nations"
Keynes, John Maynard, "The Economic Consequences of Peace"
Worth, Bonnie, "One Cent, Two Cents, Old Cent, New Cent"
Collins, Suzanne, "The Hunger Games"
Trump, Donald, "Think Like A Champion"
Piper, Watty, "The Little Engine That Could"

* * *

Other Literary Works

Charlie and the Unregulated Chocolate Factory
Where The Oligarchs Sing
A Farewell To (Your) Arms

* * *

Other Leadership Guides by C.T. Jackson

So You Want To Be A Dictator
So You Want To Be A Conspiracy Theorist
So You Want To Be A Civil War Reenactor
So You Want To Be A Vegetable
So You Want To Be An Unpublished Author
So You Want To *Be*: An Existential Guide

MEET THE AUTHOR

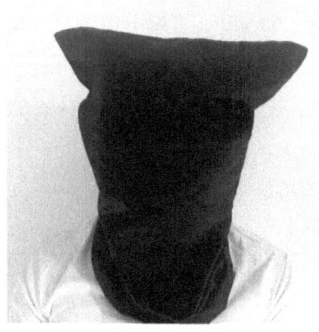

C.T. Jackson owes more than $3.5 million in bridge loans to several international banks. He has no intention of paying these loans back and has already spent the money on poor investments in the Juicero cold press juicer. (He really thought those were going to take off.) Mr. Jackson is currently being held in a gilded cage at the Intercontinental Hotel in Davos, Switzerland. When he is not laundering his Amazon book royalties, he spends his time avoiding prison with his wife in Frankfurt, Germany.

Acknowledgments

This book wouldn't have been possible without the minimum wage support from my family, friends, and the many, many underpaid factory hands involved.

To my wife, Melody, the majority shareholder of my love, whose infinite patience and encouragement kept me going in my writing.

To my mother, the person who didn't allow me to work in the sulfur mines at an early age, but instead forced me to write and learn. This waste of time is for her.

To my senior managers, Alex Boeckler, Timothy Albaugh, and Mike Rhea who provided me with sage advice and feedback on how to further the exploitation in this book.

To Paul Hawkins, whose illustrations and early corroboration turned this book from a measly start-up to a Fortune 500 juggernaut. I promise I'll pay him some day.

To the major CEOs and owners of multinational corporations, thank you for making massive profits without hurting anyone or any part of the environment.

If you would also like to be a part of the acknowledgements - please send your donation to C.T. Jackson Publishing Corporation.

Finally, to you dear reader. The rich and powerful seem to get the last laugh often, this is a way to take that back after they have taken so much from us.